BE A
CH ER

Guide

Dr Sharon Parry

First published in Great Britain in 2012 by
Need2Know
Remus House
Coltsfoot Drive
Peterborough
PE2 9BF
Telephone 01733 898103
Fax 01733 313524
www.need2knowbooks.co.uk

Contents

Not all childminders have to be registered. There are different criteria and arrangements for registering as a childminder in England, Wales, Scotland and Northern Ireland. Clear flow diagrams for deciding if you need to register and how to go about it in each of the principalities are given in chapters 2, 3, 4 and 5.

The term 'childminding' is also defined slightly differently by the registering bodies. However, a common element is the care of one or more children, for more than a total of two hours a day on domestic premises for reward.

According to the National Childminding Association (NCMA) there are around 67,000 registered childminders in England and Wales. (Source: www.ncma. org, accessed 25 April 2012).

Partnerships

Some childminders choose to work alone. Some have formed partnerships and work with another childminder in one of their homes. Some childminders have paid or unpaid assistants.

Specialisation and respite care

Some specialise in caring for children with disabilities. Others work for care organisations (e.g. local authorities) rather than directly with parents. More details of this are given in chapter 9.

What sort of people become childminders?

Childminding is a popular option for many women who wish to stay at home with their own pre-school children but who also need an income. However, it becomes a long-term career choice for many. According to the National Childminding Association 'Annual Membership Survey Report' for 2011, a third of members have been registered for ten years. The same survey showed that the majority were women aged 35 years or over but only one percent of childminders were male. There were childminders from all ethnic backgrounds. Very few childminders considered themselves to be disabled (one percent).

'Childminding is a popular option for many women who wish to stay at home with their own pre-school children but who also need an income.'

What are the advantages and disadvantages of becoming a childminder?

For many, childminding is a truly rewarding and varied career. However, it is not for everyone and the advantages and disadvantages should be carefully weighed up before you start out.

Advantages

The main advantages are:

- You are your own boss; you run your business from home and choose the hours that you work and the services that you provide.

- If you have pre-school children of your own, you can look after them at the same time and the presence of other children can provide a stimulating environment for your own.

- If you have older children, you will be available to drop them off and pick them up from school and you will be available during school holidays or if they are not well enough to attend school.

- You will have a sense of achievement knowing that you have made an important contribution to the growth and development of the children in your care.

- The work is very varied; no two days are the same. You will get plenty of fresh air and exercise and get out and about in your local community.

- You can incorporate real-life learning experiences for the children into some of your household tasks, such as shopping, gardening and cooking.

- You will have opportunities to gain additional knowledge and skills through training. Training is covered in detail in chapter 9.

- The qualifications and experience of running your own business will not only boost your confidence but will also be valued by future employers should you decide to develop alternative careers.

- There are opportunities for you to meet other carers and childminders through local support networks and to become as actively involved as you want to in local care networks and organisations. Some childminders, particularly those who work with children with special needs, liaise closely with healthcare and social care professionals. Opportunities for this sort of specialisation are covered further in chapter 9.

Disadvantages

The main disadvantages are:

- You are working from home and will be on your own with young children for at least part of the day. If you are used to working in a busy office or shop this will be a very different working environment for you.

- There is a commitment in time (training) and, to a small extent, money before you start.

- There is a rigorous registration and inspection process in place to protect the children in your care; you have to be disciplined and organised enough to complete the training and maintain all the policies and paperwork that will be required of you.

- When you have other children in your care, your children will not have you to themselves. It is important to ensure, if they are old enough, that they understand the implications of that. If they are very young, it is important that you are sure your child has the personality to be able to cope with the presence of other children in their home. However, because you choose the hours that you work, you are in control of this.

Why do parents choose childminders as their childcare?

The choice of suitable childcare is a huge issue for all parents. Childminders are a popular choice. This is because childminders can offer:

- A homely environment where children can enjoy real-life experiences such as cooking, gardening, caring for pets and trips out.

- Spontaneous activities and outings that can take advantage of the weather conditions (e.g. taking a walk in Wellingtons if it's snowing) or ties in with something the child has developed an interest in (e.g. a toy that they've brought from home).

- Fewer children per adult and the same adult every day! This helps some children cope with the separation from their parents much better than in more institutional settings such as nurseries.

- Care in the child's own neighbourhood so they can play in local parks and attend local playgroups and soft plays with other children from their own communities.

- Care for mixed age ranges. This means that once a pre-school child starts school, the same childminder can do their school pick-up giving continuity of care and a familiar face at what is sometimes a stressful time. It also means that older and younger siblings can be looked after by the same person making drop-offs and collections a lot simpler and quicker for parents.

- Flexible childcare arrangements. Some parents only require one half day a week. Others need evening, early morning or weekend care to tie in with shift work. Some parents only require term-time care whilst others only need school holidays. Many childminders are able to offer this facility.

- Childcare provided by registered childminders may be eligible for the childcare element of the Working Tax Credit. The amount received towards childcare costs is, of course, income dependent.

- Childcare vouchers can be used to pay registered childminders. Parents do not have to pay tax or national insurance contributions on the first proportion. More details on payment by childcare vouchers is given in chapter 8.

Who is suitable to become a childminder?

As part of the pre-registration checks you are required to declare anything that might prevent you working with children and present evidence of your identity and suitability for security checks. Registering authorities will check the people who live or work with you also. You will have to demonstrate that you have the knowledge and resources to provide a high standard of care and keep up with changes in the guidelines.

You will also have to demonstrate that your home is suitable and safe.

How are childminders regulated?

Childminders are regulated by the appropriate regulatory authority for England, Wales, Scotland and Northern Ireland. Childminders are regularly inspected and there are clear procedures for making complaints about childminders that fail to provide adequate care for children. Details of the regulatory process are given in chapter 6. Inspection reports are made public.

Also, parents frequently choose a childminder based on personal recommendation from other parents so consistently high standards need to be maintained.

Why do childminders have to be registered and regulated?

Regulation and registration were put in place to protect children and to reassure parents. They safeguard the health, safety and wellbeing of children and ensure that they receive high-quality care where they can achieve well, learn and develop.

Is registration the same for England, Wales, Scotland and Northern Ireland?

The registration criteria and process differ in England, Wales, Scotland and Northern Ireland. It is obviously essential to follow the correct procedure for your area and to use the correct application forms. The application process in each of the areas is covered separately.

'Childminders are regularly inspected and there are clear procedures for making complaints about childminders that fail to provide adequate care for children.'

Summing Up

- Childminders work in their own homes looking after other people's children.

- There are several different categories of childminder. Most, but not all, are required to be registered with a regulatory authority.

- Some childminders work alone, privately, for parents. Others form partnerships with other childminders. There are also opportunities for specialisation (e.g. caring for children with disabilities) and to join local care networks.

- The majority of childminders are women aged 35 years and over. However, this should not put off younger women, men and people with disabilities considering it as a career.

- A career as a childminder is an attractive career option. You will be available to look after your own children; you will be your own boss and you will have the opportunity to take additional training.

- You will also have to consider the disadvantages before you make your decision. Make sure that all your family is happy for your home to be used in this way. Be certain that you can manage the paperwork and procedures that you will be required to follow.

Chapter Two

When and How
to Register as a
Childminder – England

Registration

Who do childminders register with?

Childminders in England are registered by Ofsted. This official regulatory body inspects and regulates a vast array of childcare providers, including childminders, such as: children's centres, state and independent schools, pre-schools and nurseries through to further education colleges.

Do I need to register as a childminder?

You will need to register as a childminder if you satisfy certain criteria. The flow diagram on the following page will guide you through determining whether you should be registered as a childminder or not. If the flow diagram indicates that you do not need to register as a childminder it is likely that you will be required to register as a different type of childcarer, such as a childcare provider on domestic premises or as a nursery or a playgroup. Advice on this is available from Ofsted and the contact details are given in the help list. You should always consult them before deciding that you do not need to register.

'Childminders in England are registered by Ofsted.'

What happens if I should register but don't?

There are laws that control the provision of childcare in England (Childcare Act 2006). If you should register but don't, you could be committing an offence and may be prosecuted.

Start

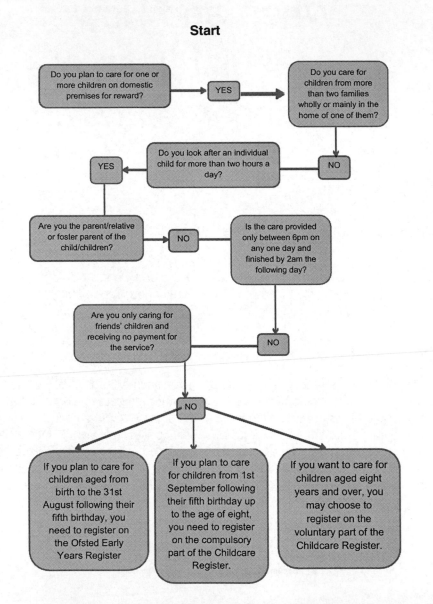

What does registration involve?

The process of becoming a childminder is fairly formal. It is essential for the safety and wellbeing of children that all the necessary checks are made and procedures followed. Having said that, there is plenty of advice, help and support available for you, and Ofsted and your local authority have knowledgeable staff who can help you through the process. You will have to show that your childminding service can meet a set of required standards.

What are the required standards that my service has to meet?

You will need to register on the Early Years Register if you fulfil the criteria outlined above and plan to care for children from birth to the 31st August following their fifth birthday. The required standards are found in the Early Years Foundation Stage.

You will need to apply to register on the Childcare Register if you fulfil the criteria outlined above and plan to care for children from the 1st September following their fifth birthday up to eight years of age.

You can voluntarily register on the Childcare Register if you plan to care for children aged eight years to 18 years.

Can I apply for both the Early Years Register and the Childcare Register at the same time?

Yes you can and many childminders do. This allows them to care for children of a range of ages. If you wish to apply for both you should use the Early Years Registration forms and you will only have to pay one fee. Section F of the EYC form allows you to indicate this.

The Childcare Register is not linked to the delivery of the Early Years Foundation Stage.

'The process of becoming a childminder is fairly formal.'

What is the Early Years Foundation Stage?

It is the statutory framework for the early education and care of children aged from birth to the 31st August following their fifth birthday. The Early Years Foundation Stage (EYFS) includes standards for young children's welfare, learning and development as well as good practice guidance.

What is the Childcare Register?

The requirements for the Childcare Register are set out in the Ofsted document *Requirements for the Childcare Register: childminders and home childcarers. A childcare factsheet*. They cover:

* The welfare and safeguarding of the children being cared for.

* The suitability of the persons in contact with the children.

* The premises and equipment.

* How the childcare provision is organised.

* The procedures for dealing with complaints.

* Record keeping and provision of information.

* Reporting incidents.

* Insurance.

* The certificate of registration.

What should I do first?

Contact the main organisations involved in providing support to would-be childminders and follow the advice that they give you. They are:

* Your local Family Information Service (FIS). You can look them up in your telephone directory or ask at your local library for their contact details or locate them online using the 'Find your FIS' facility at: http://findyourfis.daycaretrust.org.uk/kb5/findyourfis/home.page.

- Your local authority. You can look them up in your telephone directory or ask at your local library.

- The National Childminding Association (NCMA). The contact details are given in the help list.

What help can they give me?

They can:

- Arrange for you to attend a pre-registration briefing session in your local area, there is no obligation to apply at this stage. The Ofsted pre-registration briefing for those wishing to become a childminder is also available at: www.ncma.org.uk/pdf/CM%20presentation.pdf.

- Advise you how to access a paediatric first-aid course if you have not already done so.

- Provide you with all the local information you need on how to make an application and access training.

- Provide you with an application pack.

What documents or advice booklets should I read for registering on the Early Years Register?

You should read the following:

- The Ofsted guidance document *Guide to Registration on the Early Years Register: childminders*. It is available online at www.ofsted.gov.uk or from Ofsted using the contact details in the help list.

- *Statutory Framework for the Early Years Foundation Stage*. This is available from your local authority. You must read this carefully before you apply because during the registration process your ability to meet the requirements of it will be assessed.

- NCMA leaflets and advice on applying to register as a childminder in England (www.ncma.co.uk).

What documents or advice booklets should I read for registering on the Childcare Register?

You should read the following:

- *Requirements for the Childcare Register: childminders and home childcarers. A childcare factsheet.* You will have to sign a declaration that you will meet these requirements so you need to know what they are! It is available online at: www.ofsted.gov.uk or from Ofsted using the contact details in the help list.

- NCMA leaflets and advice on applying to register as a childminder in England (www.ncma.co.uk).

The application process

Do I have to complete training before I apply?

You should attend an introductory childcare training course and undertake an appropriate paediatric first-aid training course. The organisations detailed previously can help you access suitable training. The NCMA recommends that all new childminders take the 'Understand How to Set Up a Home-Based Childcare Service' training. More details on training for childminders are given in chapter 9.

'You should attend an introductory childcare training course and undertake an appropriate paediatric first-aid training course.'

How does pre-registration training help me?

The course will:

- Provide you with support and information on how to provide a good childminding service.

- Give you a chance to meet others who are applying for registration.

- Provide you with knowledge.

- Provide opportunities to ask for help and guidance.

How do I submit an application?

Application forms are part of an application pack that is available from your local FIS or online at www.ofsted.gov.uk. If you decide to apply in paper, you complete the application form and post it to Ofsted using the envelopes provided. You can also print off a paper version (Word or PDF format) from the Ofsted website.

If you would prefer to complete the form onscreen, there is a facility for you to do this but you would then need to print it off, sign it and then post it as above.

You do have an option of completing and submitting the form online via the Ofsted website. To do this you will need a government Gateway Account and you can register for one of these at: https://online.ofsted.gov.uk/OnlineOfsted/default.aspx.

Keep a copy of everything you submit!

What information do I have to provide for Early Years registration?

You have to provide a great deal of information by completing several forms and supplying other documents to support your application.

The application form

The application form (EYC form) itself is 26 pages long and requires:

- Personal information and contact details for yourself.

- Past registration details.

- Details about the care service that you intend to provide.

- Your experience and/or training in childcare.

- Your employer (if any) and two further referees.
- Details on anyone else who will be working with you and who lives with you, including children.
- Details of your suitability or disqualification.

EY2 forms for people who live with you

When you submit your EYC form to Ofsted, they will acknowledge your application and supply you with the correct number of EY2 forms. Anyone who lives with you and is over 16 or intends working with you will have to submit an EY2 form. There are also two EY2 forms in the application pack. EY2 forms are 26 pages long and require:

- Personal information and contact details.
- The connection with the registration.
- Details of past registration or childcare experience.
- Health details and referees (only for those who will be working with the children).
- Details of suitability and disqualification.
- Consent to checks that are needed to assess suitability to be in regular contact with children. These will vary according to the personal circumstances.

EY2 forms can be submitted in paper or using the electronic method mentioned previously. Everyone completing the forms consents to checks that Ofsted need to complete to assess the suitability of the would-be childminder and those who live or work with them. These checks will vary according to the applicant's personal circumstances.

Health Declaration booklet

You also have to complete a Health Declaration booklet. This will be provided in your application pack and is also available from the Ofsted website (http://www.ofsted.gov.uk/resources/childcare-registration-form-health-declaration-booklet). The booklet is sixteen pages long and you have to provide:

- Your personal details.

- Details of any medical problems that you have.

- Medication that you are taking and treatment that you have received in the past.

- Your height and weight.

- Details of smoking and alcohol consumption.

You then need to take the booklet to your GP who will have to verify the information that you have given and supply further details of any problems with your physical or mental health that could affect your registration. Your GP forwards the booklet directly to Ofsted. Some GPs may make a charge for doing this.

Checks on criminal records

Ofsted have to ensure that you and anyone who lives or works with you are suitable to be in contact with young children. Therefore, a further check has to be made on criminal records. You will be sent forms so that you can consent to these checks. Details of the checks and of those people who would not be deemed suitable to work with young children are included in chapter 10.

Other documents

Details of the policies, procedures and records that childminders are required to prepare are covered in chapter 7. Up-to-date information on which documents to include with your application should be obtained from Ofsted.

'Ofsted have to ensure that you and anyone who lives or works with you are suitable to be in contact with young children.'

What information do I have to provide for Childcare Register registration?

You have to provide a great deal of information by completing several forms and supplying other documents to support your application.

The application form

The application form (CR1 form) itself is 47 pages long but don't worry, many sections are not relevant to childminders. It requires:

* Personal information and contact details on yourself.

* Whether you are applying for the compulsory or voluntary part of the register.

* Details of the premises.

* Details about the care service that you intend to provide.

* Details on your suitability and any disqualification.

* Details on anyone else who will be working with you and who lives with you, including children.

* A reminder that childminders must have public liability insurance in their own name.

* Declarations relating to the requirements of the Childcare Register that you have to sign.

* Your consent to the checks that are needed to assess your suitability to become a childminder.

CR2 forms for people who live with you

Anyone who lives with you and is over 16 or intends working with you will have to submit a CR2 form. These forms are seventeen pages long and require:

* Personal information and contact details.

* The connection with the registration.

- Details of suitability and disqualification.
- Consent to the checks that are needed to assess suitability to be in regular contact with children. These will vary according to the personal circumstances.

Other documents

Details of the policies, procedures and records that childminders are required to prepare are covered in chapter 7. Up-to-date information on which documents to include with your application should be obtained from Ofsted.

Can I get help to complete the forms?

The quantity of information seems daunting at first but if you have difficulty in completing any forms or need more information, you can access this as part of your pre-registration training; by joining the NCMA and by contacting the Ofsted helpline on 0300 123 1231.

All the forms must be filled in truthfully. Knowingly making a false or misleading statement is an offence and could affect your application.

Is there a fee to apply?

At this stage you will be asked to pay a fee. An invoice for the non-refundable fee is sent to you detailing the amount (£35 up until 31st August 2012). Details of how to pay will also be sent. There is an online payment system where debit and credit cards can be used at: http://online.ofsted.gov.uk/onlineofsted/Default.aspx.

How long does it take?

Ofsted aims to complete the application within twelve weeks of receiving all the forms, documents and the fee. However, this is not always possible if further information needs to be collected from other people or agencies.

Pre-registration inspection

You will receive a pre-registration visit from an Ofsted inspector. They will telephone you before the visit to confirm the date and time and will show you their proof of identity (including a photograph) when they arrive.

What will happen during the pre-registration visit?

The inspector will interview you, check documents and look at your premises and equipment.

What will I be asked during the interview?

'You will receive a pre-registration visit from an Ofsted inspector.'

During the interview the inspector will assess your suitability to be a childminder and your ability to deliver the welfare, learning and development elements of the Early Years Foundation Stage. This will include questions on:

- How you will provide good outcomes for children.
- How you will identify risks to health and safety and minimise them.
- Your processes for vetting people who have contact with the children.
- How your educational programmes tie in with the early learning goals.
- How your planned activities will meet the children's needs.
- How you will observe the children and assess their progress.
- How you will meet the needs of all children including those with learning difficulties and disabilities and language needs.
- How you will make children feel valued and make a positive contribution.

How should I prepare for the interview?

You should obtain and study a copy of the Early Years Foundation Stage Pack which contains the Statutory Framework for the Early Years Foundation Stage; Practice Guidance for the Early Years Foundation Stage; a CD-ROM; a poster and cards. You can get this from the Department for Education on 0870 000

2288 or you can download them from www.education.gov.uk. You should obtain a copy of the booklet *Early Years Register – Preparing for Your Registration* http://www.ofsted.gov.uk/resources/childcare-registration-form-early-years-register-preparing-for-your-registration-visit. Read the booklet carefully and then use the pack to help you answer the questions in the booklet. The questions are not meant to be a definitive list of questions that you will be asked, but rather a way of encouraging you to think about how you will demonstrate that you can deliver the Early Years Foundation Stage to the children in your care.

What documents will be checked?

The inspector will check:

- Evidence of your identity (passport, marriage certificates).

- Two pieces of evidence of your address (utility bills/bank statements).

- Evidence of any childcare qualifications or childminder training that you have attended.

- Your paediatric first-aid certificate that covers children and young people.

- Your driver's licence, motor insurance and MOT certificates for any vehicle that you intend using for transporting children.

- Any information for prospective parents or documentation that you have already prepared.

What will they look for at my premises?

The inspector will look at all of the premises (rooms and outdoor space) and equipment that you intend to use for childminding. They will be assessing the following types of issues:

- Have all the potential risks to the children been identified, assessed and minimised?

- Are there measures to prevent children leaving the premises unsupervised?

- Are there appropriate child locks and gates?

'During the interview the inspector will assess your suitability to be a childminder and your ability to deliver the welfare, learning and development elements of the Early Years Foundation Stage.'

- Is the furniture suitable?

- Is the equipment (such as fireguards, high chairs and potties) suitable?

- Are the toys and materials suitable?

You do not have to buy a huge amount of equipment but you will need to demonstrate how you will get enough equipment for the children and how you will organise the premises to successfully deliver the Early Years Foundation Stage and provide opportunities for outdoor play. Many areas operate 'toy libraries' where childminders are able to borrow toys. You can find out details of these from your local Family Information Service.

What happens if something is not right during the registration visit?

The inspector will talk to you about any issues during your visit and send a letter confirming the action that you have to take. You may be asked to change equipment or premises or you may need to change your approach or policies. You will be given a time limit, usually two to three weeks, in which to take the action. Another visit may be carried out to check that the action has been completed.

What happens after the visit?

Once the inspector is satisfied that your application is complete and that all the checks on yourself and those working or living with you have been made, a decision is taken about your registration.

What happens if I change my mind and no longer want to register?

You can inform Ofsted that you wish to withdraw your application but the fee is non-refundable. It is better to do this than to not bother meeting all the requirements and getting your application refused as this disqualifies you from providing childcare in the future. However, if Ofsted have already sent you a notice of intention to refuse your registration, it is too late for you to withdraw, although Ofsted may allow you to do so if you explain your reasons.

What happens if my registration is granted?

If registration is granted, you will be sent a registration certificate and a *Are You Ready for Your Inspection?* booklet which has information about the inspection process and a poster giving Ofsted's contact details for parents. You must display this.

The registration always includes a condition on the number of children of different ages that you can care for. Some general information on ratios is given in chapter 10 but the final decision is down to the inspector. Other conditions may be applied.

What is the registration certificate?

This is your proof of registration and once you have received it you can start working as a childminder. It will give your registration number, the date of registration and the name of the register that you are on. It also gives your name, the address where you are allowed to provide childminding and any conditions that you have to comply with.

Your registration certificate is a legal document and must be displayed at your premises. If it gets lost or damaged, you will have to pay a fee to replace it (currently £7). It remains valid until your registration is changed, cancelled or resigned.

What happens if my registration is refused?

You will first get a legal letter, called a 'notice of intention', that sets out the reasons why Ofsted intends refusing your registration. The letter will also explain how you can object to the intention. If you do object, you must tell Ofsted that you intend to do so within fourteen days. They will consider your objections and then write to you again with a decision.

'Your registration certificate is a legal document and must be displayed at your premises.'

If the final decision is to refuse your application, you will receive a second legal letter called a 'notice of decision'. This is a serious step and it disqualifies you from providing childcare in the future.

Can I appeal against a refusal to register me?

Yes, you have the right to appeal to the Health, Education and Social Care Chamber First Tier Tribunal within three months of receiving the notice of decision. Guidance on how to appeal will be sent to you with the notice.

What if I no longer want to be a childminder?

You need to inform Ofsted by telephone or in writing that you intend to resign. They will write to you to confirm receipt.

Summing Up

- If you satisfy certain criteria you are required by law to register with Ofsted as a childminder on the Early Years Register or Childcare Register in England.

- The criteria covers the type of care you provide and the children you care for.

- Childminders are registered to protect the children that they care for and to maintain standards. The standards are contained in the Early Years Foundation Stage and in *Requirements for the Childcare Register: childminders and home childcarers. A childcare factsheet*. You should complete some basic training, including paediatric first aid before you apply.

- The application process involves you having to fill in forms, provide documents and consent to checks on you and the people who live with you.

- Your documents will be assessed and for Early Years Registration your home will be inspected and you will be interviewed.

- All of these checks are carried out in order to assess your suitability to become a childminder.

- If you are successful, you will receive a registration certificate that will set out your conditions of registration.

- If you are not successful, you will be told of the reasons why and given details on how to appeal.

Chapter Three

When and How to Register as a Childminder – Wales

Registration

Who do childminders register with?

Childminders in Wales are registered by the CSSIW. They inspect and review local authority social services and regulate and inspect social care and early years settings and agencies.

Do I need to register as a childminder?

You will need to register as a childminder if you satisfy certain criteria. The flow diagram on the following page will guide you through determining whether you should be registered as a childminder or not. If the flow diagram indicates that you do not need to register as a childminder it is likely that you will be required to register as a different type of childcarer, such as a childcare provider on domestic premises or as a nursery or a playgroup. Advice on this is available from the CSSIW and the contact details are given in the help list. You should always consult them before deciding that you do not need to register.

> 'Childminders in Wales are registered by the CSSIW.'

What happens if I should register but don't?

There are laws that control the provision of childcare in Wales: Children and Families (Wales) Measure 2010 and the Child Minding and Day Care (Wales) Regulations 2010. If you should register but don't, you could be committing an offence and may be prosecuted.

Start

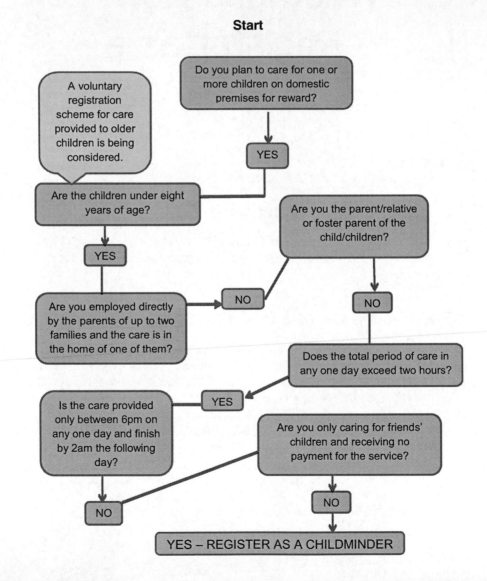

A voluntary registration scheme for care provided to older children is being considered.

Do you plan to care for one or more children on domestic premises for reward?

YES

Are the children under eight years of age?

YES

Are you the parent/relative or foster parent of the child/children?

Are you employed directly by the parents of up to two families and the care is in the home of one of them?

NO

NO

Does the total period of care in any one day exceed two hours?

Is the care provided only between 6pm on any one day and finish by 2am the following day?

YES

Are you only caring for friends' children and receiving no payment for the service?

NO

NO

YES – REGISTER AS A CHILDMINDER

What does registration involve?

The process of becoming a childminder is fairly formal. It is essential for the safety and wellbeing of children that all the necessary checks are made and procedures followed. Having said that, there is plenty of advice, help and support available for you and the CSSIW and your local authority have knowledgeable staff who can help you through the process. You will have to show that your childminding service can meet a set of required standards.

What are the required standards that my service has to meet?

The required standards are found in the Minimum Standards for Regulated Childcare in Wales 2011 which includes the Foundation Phase.

The Foundation Phase is a new approach to learning for children from three to seven years of age with an emphasis on learning by giving them more opportunities to gain first-hand experiences through play and active learning.

What should I do first?

Contact the main organisations involved in providing support to would-be childminders and follow the advice that they give you. They are:

- Your local Family Information Service (FIS). You can look them up in your telephone directory or ask at your local library for their contact details or locate them online using the 'Find your FIS' facility at: http://findyourfis.daycaretrust.org.uk/kb5/findyourfis/home.page.

- Your local authority. You can look them up in your telephone directory or ask at your local library.

- The National Childminding Association (NCMA Cymru). The contact details are given in the help list.

'The Foundation Phase is a new approach to learning for children from three to seven years of age with an emphasis on learning by giving them more opportunities to gain first-hand experiences through play and active learning.'

What help can they give me?

They can:

- Arrange for you to attend a pre-registration briefing session in your local area, there is no obligation to apply at this stage. If you are not able to access a session the help organisations listed at the end of this guide will be able to give you some initial guidance.

- Advise you how to access a paediatric first-aid course if you have not already done so.

- Provide you with all the local information you need on how to make an application and access training.

- Advise you on which pre-registration training course you should take.

What documents or advice booklets should I read?

You should read the following:

- The CSSIW guidance on applying to register as a childminder: *Childminder Information Leaflet* and *Guidance for Applicants to register as a childminder*. Both are available as part of the childminding application pack from: http://wales.gov.uk/cssiwsubsite/newcssiw/aboutus/providingsocialcare/cmreg/infoandguide/?lang=en or from the CSSIW.

- The National Minimum Standards for Regulated Childcare and The Child Minding and Day Care (Wales) Regulations 2010. They are available online at http://wales.gov.uk/docs/dhss/publications or from CSSIW using the contact details in the help list.

- NCMA Cymru leaflets and advice on applying to register as a childminder in Wales (www.ncma.co.uk).

The application process

Do I have to complete training before I apply?

Yes, the CSSIW guidance is clear that you have to complete a pre-registration training course and a paediatric first-aid training course before you can become registered. The organisations detailed on the previous page can help you access suitable training

How does pre-registration training help me?

In Wales, the pre-registration training will:

- Provide you with support and information on how to provide a good childminding service.
- Give you a chance to meet others who are applying for registration.
- Provide contact with your National Childminding Association representative and/or Local Authority Early Years Partnership development worker
- Provide information on start-up grants available to you in your area.
- Provide you with knowledge.
- Give you help and guidance in completing the application forms in the application pack.

How do I submit an application?

Application forms are part of an application pack that is available from the CSSIW in paper form or you can print off an application form at the CSSIW website and fill it in by hand. If you would prefer to complete the form onscreen, there is a facility for you to do this but you would then need to print it off, sign it and then submit as a paper copy.

The form and all relevant supporting documentation (there is a checklist on the application form) have to be submitted to your regional CSSIW office. There are four regional offices based in the east, south, west and north of Wales and

'The CSSIW guidance is clear that you have to complete a pre-registration training course and a paediatric first-aid training course before you can become registered.'

the locations are detailed in the help list. Currently, you cannot submit the forms electronically. The CSSIW encourage you to make an appointment to present your application in person at the office. You should take the following documents with you to confirm your identity:

* Proof of your identity, e.g. passport, photo driving licence etc.

* Your birth certificate.

* A recent photograph of yourself.

Keep a copy of everything you submit!

What information do I have to provide?

You have to provide a great deal of information by completing several forms and supplying other documents to support your application.

The application form

The application form itself is 52 pages long and consists of several parts. Part 1 requires:

* Personal information and contact details for yourself.

* Your experience and qualifications in childcare and previous employment.

* Two referees.

* Details of previous registrations and disqualifications.

* Details about the care service that you intend to provide and the premises where it will be provided.

* Details on anyone else who will be working with you and who lives with you, including children.

Part 2 of the form requires you to demonstrate that you will fulfil the requirements of the standards outlined above. The sections of the form are:

* Information on service.

* Planning for individual needs and preferences.

- Empowering service users.
- Encouraging lifestyle choices.
- Quality of care.
- Staffing.
- Conduct and management of the service.
- Complaints, protection and other significant events.
- The physical environment.

Forms for people who live with you

Appendix 2 has to be completed by anyone who lives with you and is aged over 16 or intends working with you. It requires personal information and contact details; previous addresses; declaration of supervision orders or disqualifications. Everyone completing the forms consents to checks that the CSSIW need to complete to assess the suitability of the would-be childminder and those who live or work with them. These checks will vary according to the applicant's personal circumstances.

Health information

Appendix 1 has to be taken to your GP who has to review your medical notes and sign a declaration that you are physically and mentally fit to look after children under the age of eight.

Checks on criminal records

The CSSIW have to ensure that you, and anyone who lives or works with you, are suitable to be in contact with young children. Therefore, a further check has to be made on criminal records. You will be sent forms so that you can consent to these checks. Details of the checks and of those people who would not be deemed suitable to work with young children are included in chapter 10.

Other documents

Appendix 3 is a fire safety checklist for you to complete to inform the CSSIW of the results of the fire safety assessment of your premises. Based on this information, the CSSIW may decide that a fire officer should be consulted or should visit your home.

Details of the policies, procedures and records that childminders are required to prepare are covered in chapter 7. Up-to-date information on which documents to include with your application should be obtained from the CSSIW.

'The quantity of information seems daunting at first but if you have difficulty in completing any forms you will be given support in the pre-registration training.'

Can I get help to complete the forms?

The quantity of information seems daunting at first but if you have difficulty in completing any forms you will be given support in the pre-registration training.

All the forms must be filled in truthfully. Knowingly making false or misleading statements is an offence and could affect your application.

Is there a fee to apply?

There is currently no fee to apply for registration in Wales.

How long does it take?

The length of the application process is variable and the CSSIW do not give any estimations.

Pre-registration inspection

You will receive a pre-registration visit from a CSSIW inspector. They will telephone you before the visit to confirm the date and time and will show you their proof of identity (including a photograph) when they arrive.

What will happen during the pre-registration visit?

The inspector will interview you, check documents and look at your premises and equipment.

What will I be asked during the interview?

During the interview the inspector will assess your suitability to be a childminder and your ability to deliver the National Minimum Standards for Regulated Childcare. This will include questions on:

- Your proposed way of working.
- The things that you have written in your application form.
- Your previous study, work and qualifications.
- Your understanding of your responsibilities as a registered childminder.
- Your systems to assess and introduce children into your care.
- Your systems of providing suitable activities and experiences for them.
- The ways in which you will promote and make proper provision for the welfare of the children you care for.
- How you intend to select and assess any assistants you may want to employ, the records you must keep about them and how you will supervise their work.
- How you will manage, monitor and develop the quality of your service.
- How you will involve parents and children in that process.
- How you will securely store your records.

How should I prepare for the interview?

You should read over the documents listed previously and your application form and all the documents that you submitted with it.

What documents will be checked?

The inspector will check:

- Evidence of any childcare qualifications or childminder training that you have attended.

- Your first-aid certificate that covers children and young people.

- Your identity documents, if you did not present them when you submitted your application.

- The supporting documents sent with your application form (see chapter 7).

What will they look for at my premises?

'The inspector will look at all of the premises (rooms and outdoor space) and equipment that you intend to use for childminding.'

The inspector will look at all of the premises (rooms and outdoor space) and equipment that you intend to use for childminding. They will be assessing the following types of issues:

- The safety and security of your premises.

- Maintenance and regular inspection of your appliances.

- Fire safety guidance.

- Guarding hot surfaces, safety glass, trip, fall, electrical and chemical hazards.

- Controlling outdoor hazards such as fences, greenhouses, garden chemicals, vehicles and animals.

- Arrangements for first aid.

- The suitability of the premises and outdoor spaces where childminding is to be provided.

- Identification of any hazards and installing suitable safety measures.

You do not have to buy a huge amount of equipment but you will need to demonstrate how you will get enough equipment for the children and how you will organise the premises to successfully deliver the required standards for care and learning and provide opportunities for outdoor play. Many areas operate 'toy libraries' where childminders are able to borrow toys. You can find out details of these from your local Family Information Service.

What happens if something is not right during the registration visit?

The inspector will talk to you about them during your visit and send a letter confirming the action that you have to take. Once they are done you should send written confirmation to the inspector.

What happens after the visit?

Once the inspector is satisfied that your application is complete and that all the checks on yourself and those working or living with you have been made, your application will be presented to a CSSIW Team Manager for a decision on registration.

What happens if I change my mind and no longer want to register?

You can inform CSSIW that you wish to withdraw your application

What happens if my registration is granted?

If registration is granted, you will be sent a registration certificate.

The registration always includes a condition on the number of children of different ages that you can care for. Other conditions may be applied.

What is the registration certificate?

This is your proof of registration and once you have received it you can start working as a childminder. It will give your registration number and the date of registration. It also gives your name, the address where you are allowed to

'The registration always includes a condition on the number of children of different ages that you can care for.'

provide childminding and any conditions that you have to comply with. Your registration certificate is a legal document and must be displayed at your premises.

What happens if my registration is refused?

If the intention is to refuse your application, you will be issued with a 'Notice of Intention to Refuse Registration' and you have 28 days in which to make any oral or written objections before a decision is finally made.

If you choose not to make any objections or, after consideration of any objections you make, CSSIW decide to refuse to grant you registration, you will be issued with a 'Notice of Decision to Refuse Registration'.

Can I appeal against a refusal to register me?

You have a period of three months to appeal to the First Tier Tribunal.

What if I no longer want to be a childminder?

You need to inform CSSIW by telephone or in writing that you intend to resign and they will write to you to confirm receipt.

Summing Up

- If you satisfy certain criteria you are required by law to register with CSSIW as a childminder.

- The criteria covers the type of care you provide and the children you care for.

- Childminders are registered to protect the children that they care for and to maintain standards. The standards are contained in the National Minimum Standards.

- You should complete some basic training, including paediatric first-aid training before you apply.

- The application process involves you having to fill in forms, provide documents and consent to checks on you and the people who live with you.

- Your home will be inspected, your documents will be assessed and you will be interviewed.

- All of these checks are carried out in order to assess your suitability to become a childminder.

- If you are successful, you will receive a registration certificate that will set out your conditions of registration.

- If you are not successful, you will be told of the reasons why and given details on how to appeal.

Chapter Four

When and How to Register as a Childminder – Scotland

Registration

Who do childminders register with?

Childminders in Scotland are registered by the Care Inspectorate. The Care Inspectorate are the independent body that exists to regulate and promote improvement in care and children's services.

Do I need to register as a childminder?

You will need to register as a childminder if you satisfy certain criteria. The flow diagram on the following page will guide you through determining whether you should be registered as a childminder or not. If the flow diagram indicates that you do not need to register as a childminder it is likely that you will be required to register as a different type of childcarer, such as a childcare provider on domestic premises or as a nursery or a playgroup. Advice on this is available from the Care Inspectorate and the contact details are given in the help list. You should always consult them before deciding that you do not need to register.

'Childminders in Scotland are registered by the Care Inspectorate.'

What happens if I should register but don't?

There are laws that control the provision of childcare in Scotland, The Public Services Reform (Scotland) Act 2010. If you should register but don't, you could be committing an offence and may be prosecuted.

Start

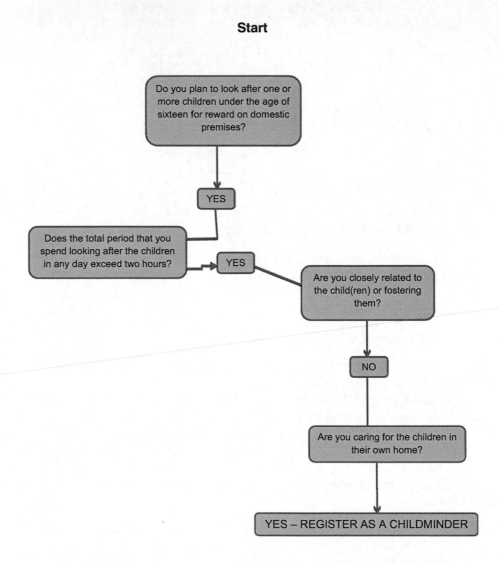

Do you plan to look after one or more children under the age of sixteen for reward on domestic premises?

YES

Does the total period that you spend looking after the children in any day exceed two hours?

YES

Are you closely related to the child(ren) or fostering them?

NO

Are you caring for the children in their own home?

YES – REGISTER AS A CHILDMINDER

What does registration involve?

The process of becoming a childminder is fairly formal. It is essential for the safety and wellbeing of children that all the necessary checks are made and procedures followed. Having said that, there is plenty of advice, help and support available for you and the Care Inspectorate and your local authority have knowledgeable staff who can help you through the process. You will have to show that your childminding service can meet a set of required standards.

What are the required standards that my service has to meet?

The required standards are found in the *National Care Standards for Early Education and Childcare up to the age of 16*. These are the expected minimum standards for early years education and childcare that have been set by the Scottish government.

What should I do first?

Contact the main organisations involved in providing support to would-be childminders and follow the advice that they give you. They are:

- The Care Inspectorate.
- The Scottish Childminding Association at www.childminding.org or call them on 01786 445377.

What help can they give me?

They can:

- Advise you how to access a paediatric first-aid course if you have not already done so.
- Provide you with all the local information you need on how to make an application and access training.

'There is plenty of advice, help and support available for you and the Care Inspectorate and your local authority have knowledgeable staff who can help you through the process.'

What documents or advice booklets should I read?

You should read the following:

- *National Care Standards for Early Education and Childcare up to the age of 16*. You can obtain this online from www.scotland.gov.uk or you can order a printed copy from *Scottish Government Titles* at the address given in the help list. The document is free but there will be a small charge for postage.

- The laws that apply to childminding in Scotland by clicking on 'The Law' tab on the Care Inspectorate's website www.careinspectorate.com.

- The booklets that have been produced for childminders by the Care Inspectorate namely: *Applying to Register a Care Service: Guidance for Providers* and *Childminders: What to Expect When We Inspect,* they are available on their website, www.careinspectorate.com.

- Advice published by the Scottish Childminding association (SCMA).

- The Scottish Social Services Council (SSSC) have Codes of Conduct for people involved in caring professions. Childminders do not have to be registered with SSSC but it is considered good practice to adhere to these codes of conduct and the Care Inspectorate will consider the requirements of these codes when they are inspecting you. They can be downloaded from the SSSC website: http://www.sssc.uk.com/component/option,com_docman/Itemid,486/gid,1020/task,doc_details/.

'The Scottish Childminding Association runs induction training for people who are considering applying to register as a childminder.'

The application process

Do I have to complete training before I apply?

The Care Inspectorate encourages applicants to take advantage of local training before and during the application process.

How does pre-registration training help me?

The Scottish Childminding Association runs induction training for people who are considering applying to register as a childminder. The course will:

- Provide you with support and information on how to provide a good childminding service.

- Give you a chance to meet others who are applying for registration.

- Provide you with knowledge.

- Provide opportunities to ask for help and guidance.

- Give you help and guidance in completing the application to become a childminder.

How do I submit an application?

Application forms are available on the Care Inspectorate's website, you can complete them onscreen and you are encouraged to apply online at www. scswis.com. You can request a paper version of the application pack by contacting the Care Inspectorate National Enquiries Line (0845 600 9527). Details of where to return the paper forms are included.

What information do I have to provide?

You have to provide a great deal of information by completing several forms and supplying other documents to support your application. Parts 1-4 of the application form require:

- Personal information and contact details for yourself.

- Your experience and qualifications in childcare.

- Two referees who cannot be relatives (where you have been employed by one employer for longer than three months in the last five years, one of your references must be from them).

- Information about the domestic premises (your home) where the childminding service will be provided and a declaration that it is suitable for that purpose.

- Statements and disclosures relating to your fitness and suitability.

- Details about how your childminding service will be provided and evaluated.

- Your policies and procedures.

- Your demonstration that you will fulfil the requirements of the standards outlined above.

Forms for people who live with you

You will have to provide details of everyone (including children) that live in your home on a regular basis with you so that they can be checked for their suitability to be around young children. Everyone completing the forms consents to checks that the Care Inspectorate need to complete to assess the suitability of the would-be childminder and those who live or work with them.

Health information

You will have to provide information on your fitness to become a childminder.

Checks on criminal records

The Care Inspectorate have to ensure that you and anyone who lives or works with you are suitable to be in contact with young children. Therefore, a further check has to be made on criminal records. You will be sent forms so that you can consent to these checks. Details of the checks and of those people who would not be deemed suitable to work with young children are included in chapter 10.

Other documents

Details of the policies, procedures and records that childminders are required to prepare are covered in chapter 7. Up-to-date information on which documents to include with your application should be obtained from the Care Inspectorate.

Can I get help to complete the forms?

The quantity of information seems daunting at first but if you have difficulty in completing any forms or need more information, you can access this as part of your pre-registration training; by joining the SCMA and by contacting the Care Inspectorate.

All the forms must be filled in truthfully. Knowingly making a false or misleading statement is an offence and could affect your application

Is there a fee to apply?

Yes, there is a non-returnable application fee. You will be sent an invoice for this. This fee includes the cost of a Protection of Vulnerable Groups (PVG) Scheme record check for you and Disclosure Scotland criminal records checks or their equivalents for all your adult family members living with you. The fee is currently £28. The fee can be paid by debit or credit card over the telephone or online; by bank transfer; by cheque or postal order with a payment slip or by cash at a Care Inspectorate office.

How long does it take?

It takes between six weeks and six months for all the checks to be completed.

Pre-registration inspection

You will receive a pre-registration visit from a Care Inspectorate inspector.

What will happen during the pre-registration visit?

The inspector will interview you, check documents and look at your premises and equipment.

What will I be asked during the interview?

During the interview the inspector will assess your suitability to be a childminder and your ability to deliver the National Care Standards for Early Education and Childcare up to the age of 16. This will include questions on:

- The ways in which you will meet the needs of the children in your care.

- How you will protect their health and safety.

- How you will plan suitable activities for them.

How should I prepare for the interview?

You should read over the documents listed previously and your application form and all the documents that you submitted with it.

What documents will be checked?

The inspector will check:

- Evidence of your identity (birth certificate, change of name, photographic identification).

- Insurance documents.

- Certificates for your qualifications and training.

- The supporting documents sent required for registration (see chapter 7).

What will they look for at my premises?

The inspector will look at all of the premises (rooms and outdoor space) and equipment that you intend to use for childminding. They will be assessing the following types of issues:

- Availability of toys, activities and equipment.

- Health and safety issues.

- Pets you have and how you keep them.

- Smoking arrangements.
- Provision for children with special needs.

You do not have to buy a huge amount of equipment but you will need to demonstrate how you will get enough equipment for the children and how you will organise the premises to successfully deliver the National Care Standards. Many areas operate 'toy libraries' where childminders are able to borrow toys. You can find out details of these from your local Family Information Service at www.scottishchildcare.gov.uk.

What happens if something is not right during the registration visit?

The inspector will talk to you about any issues during your visit and send a letter confirming the action that you have to take. Once they are done you should send written confirmation to the inspector.

What happens after the visit?

Once the inspector is satisfied that your application is complete and that all the checks on yourself and those working or living with you have been made, an assessment report is prepared recommending that your application is either granted or refused.

What happens if I change my mind and no longer want to register?

You can inform the Care Inspectorate in writing that you wish to withdraw your application. The application fee is non-refundable. If you withdraw your application before a decision about your registration is made, it does not affect any future applications that you wish to make.

'You do not have to buy a huge amount of equipment but you will need to demonstrate how you will get enough equipment for the children and how you will organise the premises to successfully deliver the National Care Standards.'

What happens if my registration is granted?

If registration is granted the Care Inspectorate write to you to inform you that your registration has been granted and list any conditions that are attached to the registration. It is usual for conditions such as the number and ages of children you can care for to be attached to registration but there may be other conditions as well. You need to check that all the details are correct and indicate that you agree with the conditions by returning a form. At the same time you will be asked whether you want the details of your service to be included on the childcare information service list held by your local authority. You will also be sent a list of records that you must keep and matters that you must inform the Care Inspectorate about.

Once the form has been received you will be sent your registration certificate.

What is the registration certificate?

This is your proof of registration and once you have received it you can start working as a childminder. It will give your registration number and the date of registration. It also gives your name, the address where you are allowed to provide childminding and any conditions that you have to comply with. Your registration certificate is a legal document and must be displayed at your premises. It is an offence under the Public Services Reform (Scotland) Act 2010 not to display your certificate while you are providing a childminding service.

'It is an offence under the Public Services Reform (Scotland) Act 2010 not to display your certificate while you are providing a childminding service.'

What happens if my registration is refused?

The Care Inspectorate will write to you informing you that they are refusing your application giving the reasons for doing so.

Can I appeal against a refusal to register me?

Yes, you can first appeal in writing within 14 days to the Care Inspectorate. If this is not successful you can appeal to the Sheriff within 14 days. The Sheriff's decision is final.

You can also appeal in writing against the proposed conditions within 14 days of receiving the registration letter. If this is not successful you can appeal to the Sheriff within 14 days. The Sheriff's decision is final. If you win the appeal you will be issued with a Registration Certificate. The service cannot operate until a decision is made.

If you are unhappy with the way your application has been processed or with the conduct of a Care Inspectorate inspector you can complain to The Care Inspectorate's Complaints Co-ordinator.

What if I no longer want to be a childminder?

You have to inform the Care Inspectorate using an 'application to cancel' form three months before you actually want to stop. The Care Inspectorate may agree a shorter period with you. Once your registration is cancelled you have to return your registration certificate to the Care Inspectorate.

Summing Up

- If you satisfy certain criteria you are required by law to register with the Care Inspectorate as a childminder.

- The criteria covers the type of care you provide and the children you care for.

- Childminders are registered to protect the children that they care for and to maintain standards. The standards are contained in the National Care Standards for Early Education and Childcare up to the age of 16.

- You are encouraged to complete some basic training, including paediatric first-aid training before you apply.

- The application process involves you having to fill in forms, provide documents and consent to checks on you and the people who live with you.

- Your home will be inspected, your documents will be assessed and you will be interviewed.

- All of these checks are carried out in order to assess your suitability to become a childminder.

- If you are successful, you will receive a registration certificate that will set out your conditions of registration.

- If you are not successful, you will be told of the reasons why and given details on how to appeal.

Chapter Five

When and How to Register as a Childminder – Northern Ireland

Registration

Who do childminders register with?

Childminders in Northern Ireland are registered by one of the Health and Social Services Trusts:

- Belfast Health and Social Care Trust.
- Northern Health and Social Care Trust.
- South Eastern Health and Social Care Trust.
- Southern Health and Social Care Trust.
- Western Health and Social Care Trust.

The Early Years Teams at these trusts provide guidance and advice on the individual registration procedures. Some general guidance is given overleaf.

Do I need to register as a childminder?

You will need to register as a childminder if you satisfy certain criteria. The flow diagram on the following page will guide you through determining whether you should be registered as a childminder or not. If the flow diagram indicates that you do not need to register as a childminder it is likely that you will be required to register as a different type of childcarer, such as a childcare provider on domestic premises or as a nursery or a playgroup. Advice on this is available from your local Health and Social Services Trust. The contact details are given in the help list. You should always consult them before deciding that you do not need to register.

What happens if I should register but don't?

'The registration and inspection of childminding services in Northern Ireland is governed by the Children (NI) Order 1995.'

The registration and inspection of childminding services in Northern Ireland is governed by the Children (NI) Order 1995. If you should register but don't, you could be committing an offence and may be prosecuted.

Start:

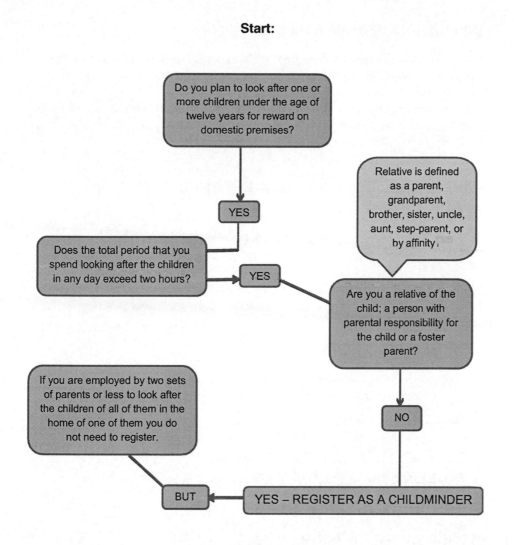

Do you plan to look after one or more children under the age of twelve years for reward on domestic premises?

YES

Does the total period that you spend looking after the children in any day exceed two hours?

YES

Relative is defined as a parent, grandparent, brother, sister, uncle, aunt, step-parent, or by affinity.

Are you a relative of the child; a person with parental responsibility for the child or a foster parent?

NO

If you are employed by two sets of parents or less to look after the children of all of them in the home of one of them you do not need to register.

BUT

YES – REGISTER AS A CHILDMINDER

What does registration involve?

The process of becoming a childminder is fairly formal. It is essential for the safety and wellbeing of children that all the necessary checks are made and procedures followed. Having said that, there is plenty of advice, help and support available for you and your local Early Years Team have knowledgeable staff that can help you through the process. You will have to show that your childminding service can meet set of required standards.

What are the required standards that my service has to meet?

The required standards are found in *The Children (NI) Order 1995 Guidance and Regulations Volume 2, Family Support, Childminding and Day Care*. They are a set of criteria that have been adopted in order to protect children, promote good standards, reassure parents and help childminders to offer a good standard of service to children and their parents.

What should I do first?

Contact the main organisations involved in providing support to would-be childminders and follow the advice that they give you. They are:

- The Early Years Team at your local Health and Social Services Trust. Contact details are given in the help list. They will be able to give you specific information.
- The Northern Ireland Childminding Association. Contact details are given in the help list.

What help can they give me?

They can:

- Advise you on any training that you will need and how to access it.
- Provide you with all the local information and support you need on how make an application.

62

What documents or advice booklets should I read?

You should read the following:

- Social Services information booklets and leaflets that give details on how to obtain an application form; the timescales involved once you apply; sources of information from other Departments; the references you will require for registration; the registration process and the appeals system. They are available from your local library or trust offices. Contact details are given in the help list.

- The NICMA has information leaflets and guidance on their website www. nicma.org.

The application process

Do I have to complete training before I apply?

Some Trusts offer pre-registration briefings. Some Trusts may also suggest that you attend a training course, e.g. a first-aid course before you register.

How does pre-registration training help me?

The pre-registration briefings and training will:

- Provide you with support and information on how to provide a good childminding service.

- Give you a chance to meet others who are applying for registration.

- Provide you with knowledge.

- Provide opportunities to ask for help and guidance.

- Give you help and guidance in completing the application to become a childminder.

'Some Trusts offer pre-registration briefings. Some Trusts may also suggest that you attend a training course eg a first aid course before you register.'

How do I submit an application?

Each Trust will provide you with their application form and details of how to submit it to them. They will also give you details of the documents and other information that you will have to provide.

What information do I have to provide?

Each Trust has their own application form. In general terms, the application forms require:

- Personal information and contact details for yourself.

- Your qualifications and experience of working with children.

- Details about your health.

- Two character references.

- References from your health visitor.

- Your permission for a Health and Social Care Trust Records check.

Forms for people who live with you

You will have to provide details of everyone (including children) that live in your home on a regular basis with you so that they can be checked for their suitability to be around young children. Everyone completing the forms consents to checks that the Trusts need to complete to assess the suitability of the would-be childminder and those who live or work with them. These checks will vary according to the applicant's personal circumstances.

Health information

You will have to provide a medical reference from your GP.

'You will have to provide details of everyone (including children) that live in your home on a regular basis with you so that they can be checked for their suitability to be around young children.'

Checks on criminal records

The Trusts have to ensure that you and anyone who lives or works with you are suitable to be in contact with young children. Therefore, a further check has to be made on criminal records. You will be sent forms so that you can consent to these checks. Details of the checks and of those people who would not be deemed suitable to work with young children are included in chapter 10.

Other documents

Details of the policies, procedures and records that childminders are required to prepare are covered in chapter 7. Up-to-date information on which documents to include with your application should be obtained from your local Trust.

Can I get help to complete the forms?

The quantity of information seems daunting at first but if you have difficulty in completing any forms you will be given support in the pre-registration training and from the Early Years Team at your local Trust.

All the forms must be filled in truthfully. Knowingly make false or misleading statements is an offence and could affect your application.

Is there a fee to apply?

There is no fee to apply.

How long does it take?

It should take no longer than three months

Pre-registration inspection

You will receive a pre-registration visit from a social worker from your Early Years Team.

What will happen during the pre-registration visit?

The social worker will interview you, check documents and look at your premises and equipment.

What will I be asked during the interview?

During the interview the social worker will assess your suitability to be a childminder and your ability to deliver care of the required standard. This will include questions on:

- Your application form.
- Your plans and ideas for childminding.
- Your ability to provide warm, consistent care.
- Your ability to treat children as individuals.
- Your health.
- Any criminal records you may have.
- Your qualifications or previous experience of looking after children.
- Your knowledge of the guidance on sharing the care with parents.
- Your knowledge of the guidance on play and speech.
- Your knowledge of the guidance on setting limits for behaviour and appropriate sanctions.
- Your knowledge of the guidance on child protection issues.
- Your knowledge of the guidance on how to react in a medical emergency and how to deal with minor injuries.

How should I prepare for the interview?

You should attend any pre-registration briefings or training that are offered and read all the documents listed previously.

What documents will be checked?

The social worker will check:

▪ Evidence of your identity.

▪ The supporting documentation that was required for the application process (see chapter 7).

What will they look for at my premises?

The social worker will look at all of the premises (rooms and outdoor space) and equipment that you intend to use for childminding. They will be assessing the following types of issues:

▪ Safety and suitability.

▪ Household safety precautions such as stairgates and safety glass.

▪ Fire precautions such as smoke detectors and fire blankets.

▪ Practical arrangements for rest periods, eating and visiting the toilet.

▪ Equipment and toys you propose to use.

You do not have to buy a huge amount of equipment but you will need to demonstrate how you will get enough equipment for the children and how you will organise the premises to successfully deliver the required standards. Many areas operate 'toy libraries' and some social services and voluntary organisations run equipment loan schemes where childminders are able to borrow toys. You can find out details of these from your local Early Years Team.

What happens if something is not right during the registration visit?

You will be told this during your visit and asked to put them right.

What happens after the visit?

Once the social worker is satisfied that your application is complete and that all the checks on yourself and those working or living with you have been made, a decision on your registration will be made.

What happens if I change my mind and no longer want to register?

You need to inform your local Trust immediately.

What happens if my registration is granted?

If registration is granted this will be confirmed in writing and you will be sent a registration certificate. There will be conditions attached to the registration including the maximum number of children that you can care for, safety matters and records.

What is the registration certificate?

This is your proof of registration and once you have received it you can start working as a childminder. It sets out the requirements of registration that should be followed at all times. The certificate should be available for parents to see.

What happens if my registration is refused?

If the intention is to refuse your application you will receive notice in writing.

Can I appeal against a refusal to register me?

Yes, you can tell social services that you want to appeal and present your reasons to a panel. If the panel agrees with you, your registration will be granted. If it does not, you can appeal to the courts.

What if I no longer want to be a childminder?

You will need to inform the Trust, by letter and return your registration certificate.

Summing Up

- If you satisfy certain criteria you are required by law to register with your local Health and Social Services Trust.

- The criteria covers the type of care you provide and the children you care for.

- Childminders are registered to protect the children that they care for and to maintain standards. The standards are contained in *The Children (NI) Order 1995 Guidance and Regulations Volume 2, Family Support, Childminding and Day Care Centre*.

- You are encouraged to complete some basic training, including paediatric first-aid training before you apply.

- The application process involves you having to fill in forms, provide documents and consent to checks on you and the people who live with you.

- Your home will be inspected, your documents will be assessed and you will be interviewed.

- All of these checks are carried out in order to assess your suitability to become a childminder.

- If you are successful, you will receive a registration certificate that will set out your conditions of registration.

- If you are not successful, you will be told of the reasons why and given details on how to appeal.

Chapter Six

Regulation of Childminders

The regulation of childminders is the responsibility of the four different regulatory authorities mentioned in the previous four chapters. Their approach to regulation differs and specific up-to-date guidance must be obtained from the appropriate authority.

Why do childminders have to be regulated?

Regulation of childcare services is important. It exists in order to:

* Protect children.

* Ensure good outcomes for children.

* Ensure that childcare providers meet the requirements of the minimum standards that apply in their area.

* Promote high quality in the provision of care and early learning.

* Provide reassurance to parents.

What does regulation mean?

In practice, regulation takes the form of registration (covered in chapters 2, 3, 4 and 5), inspection and investigation of complaints and incidents and enforcement action where necessary.

Do I have to do anything to maintain my registration?

Yes. There are several things that you have to do to keep up your registration.

Informing your regulatory authority of changes

You have to inform your regulatory authority about changes that could affect your childminding service. Some regulatory authorities have specific forms that you can use to do this. If you are not sure, always check. These include:

- Changes to your premises or facilities, for example if you alter your house or move.

- Changes to the care you provide, for example if someone comes to work with you and you want to change the number of children that you care for.

- Changes to the people who live or work with you, for example if someone moves into your household; if someone becomes 16 years of age or if someone is convicted of an offence.

- Significant events, such as injury or death of a child you are looking after.

'You have to inform your regulatory authority about changes that could affect your childminding service. Some regulatory authorities have specific forms that you can use to do this.'

Certificate conditions and annual fees

You must at all times work within the conditions set out on your certificate. In some areas you have to pay an annual fee to continue your registration.

Forms and records

You are required to keep certain records and documents. These are covered in more detail in chapter 7.

You should have a system for monitoring, reviewing and improving the quality of care you give to children and think about how you intend to improve your service each year. In some areas you have to complete an annual form giving information on how you have assessed your service. Guidance is available for completing these forms from your regulatory authority and in some cases can be submitted online. The information that you give is used before and during your inspection. These are sometimes called self-assessment forms.

Inspection

How often will I be inspected?

Newly registered childminders are usually inspected during their first year of registration. After that, the frequency of inspection varies from area to area, for example Ofsted carry out inspections every three years or so. You are more likely to be inspected if your previous inspection found problems with your service or if you are making significant changes, e.g. a change of premises. You will always be inspected if there is a complaint made against you.

Will I be given a date for the inspection?

Again, this varies between areas but on the whole you will not know exactly when the visit is going to happen. Having said that, most regulatory authorities do send out pre-inspection packs or ring beforehand to confirm your opening hours so you know an inspection is coming in the next few weeks or months. The pre-inspection packs may contain self-assessment forms and questionnaires for parents.

Is there anything I can do to prepare for the inspection?

If you are providing a consistently high-quality service and adhering to all the guidelines there is really not much more that you need to do. These tips may be helpful:

- Make sure that you complete any self-assessment forms that you are requested to submit prior to the inspection.

- Make sure that all your policies, procedures and records are up to date.

- Make sure that you have informed the regulatory authority of any changes.

'Newly registered childminders are usually inspected during their first year of registration.'

- Read any pre-inspection guidance that your regulatory authority has produced and familiarise yourself again with all the minimum standards.

- Make sure that you have addressed any points identified in your previous inspection report.

- Keep any information about how parents view your service and any improvements you have made as a result. This information will give a fuller picture of your service and help the inspector to see how well you work with parents to ensure the best outcomes for their children.

- Think about how you can demonstrate that you work with other childcare providers in your area. Be ready to show that you work with other providers and professionals from other agencies to identify children's learning needs.

'The inspector will assess the quality of the service you provide and your understanding of the requirements.'

Who are the inspectors and how will I know that they are genuine?

The inspection will be carried out by a trained regulatory authority inspector who will always show their identification card which will include a photograph of them. You must look at this before you allow them to enter. If you have concerns, you should call the appropriate regulatory authority helpline.

What happens during the inspection?

Inspections last for several hours. The inspector will assess the quality of the service you provide and your understanding of the requirements by:

- Talking to you and anyone else who works with you.

- Looking at the premises.

- Talking to parents and children (if present).

- Looking at your paperwork.

- Observing the care provided.

- Possibly leading an activity with the children.

At the end of the inspection they will give you feedback (a verbal report) and tell you if anything needs to be improved and explain what happens next. Detailed guidance on what the inspector is assessing is available from your regulatory authority but the focus of inspections is often influenced by parents, questionnaires and self-evaluation forms.

What happens after the inspection?

You will receive a letter detailing what you have to do, if anything, to retain your registration. Where there are serious concerns about the children's safety or welfare, registration can be cancelled. In serious, but very rare cases, registration is cancelled and prosecutions can be taken.

You will then receive a written report. It will focus on the strengths of the setting, areas of good practice and any areas for improvement.

The reports are public documents and you can share them with anyone you choose. You have to make them available to parents. Some regulatory authorities publish all inspection reports on their websites.

In Scotland, childminders are awarded a grade for each of three quality themes (care and support; environment and staffing; management and leadership). The grades range from 6 (excellent) to 1 (unsatisfactory).

In England, childminders are awarded a grade for three areas of the service (overall effectiveness of Early Years provision; effectiveness of leadership and management of the Early Years provision; the quality of the provision in the Early Years Foundation Stage). The grades range from 1 (outstanding and indicates that the aspect of provision is of exceptionally high quality) to 4 (inadequate and indicates that this aspect of the provision is not good enough).

Also, Ofsted run an outstanding provider scheme. Childminders who have achieved an overall grade of outstanding in their inspection are entitled to use the Ofsted outstanding provider logo on their stationery and websites. They also get a congratulatory letter personally signed by Her Majesty's Chief Inspector, an outstanding provider certificate and a CD with a copy of the Ofsted outstanding provider logo and guidance on how the logo may be used.

Will parents be able to see my inspection report?

An excellent inspection report is a superb marketing tool and you will want to share it with prospective parents. You are obliged to show the report to the parents of all children in your care. In some areas parents can also access your reports online.

What happens if there is a complaint about my service?

Complaints made about your service will be carefully and fairly investigated, and you will be inspected. If the complaint is upheld, a recommendation to take a particular action to improve your service may be made. If there are serious concerns about your service your registration can be cancelled.

'An excellent inspection report is a superb marketing tool and you will want to share it with prospective parents.'

What is meant by enforcement?

Enforcement means taking action so that a poor childminding service does not continue. This is needed to protect children. Enforcement may vary by regulatory authority, but in general if they find that a service is not good enough or is not complying with the law they can:

- Discuss the situation with you and try to resolve it.

- Re-grade your service on your inspection report.

- Impose, vary or remove a condition on the registration of the service.

- Serve an improvement notice which gives the provider a specified amount of time to improve the situation.

- Cancel the registration.

- Take urgent steps to cancel registration or to impose, vary or remove a condition on the registration of the service. This is only done when there is a serious risk to life, health or wellbeing.

There are opportunities during the enforcement process for the childminder to have their views heard and to appeal.

Summing Up

■ Childminders have to be regulated to protect the children that they look after to ensure that high standards are maintained.

■ In practice, regulation means registration, inspection, investigating complaints and enforcement.

■ To maintain registration, childminders must inform the regulatory authority of changes to their premises, the care that they provide, the people who live or work with them and any significant events.

■ Childminders also have to keep to the conditions of their registration and maintain certain records.

■ Childminders receive fairly unannounced inspections of their service. Usually, an inspector will contact them a few weeks before to confirm their opening times. The frequency of inspection varies but new childminders are inspected quite soon after registration.

■ To prepare for the inspection, childminders should read all the guidance available from their regulatory authority and keep up to date with all the forms and records.

■ During the inspection the inspector will interview you, look at the premises and inspect documents.

■ After the inspection, the inspector will outline any improvements that you need to make.

■ You will be sent a detailed inspection report.

■ The inspection report is a public document and you can show it to anyone you wish. You have to show it to the parents of the children you care for. Some regulatory authorities publish them on their websites.

■ Regulatory authorities have the power to remove your registration and serve notices if the quality of the service is very poor.

Chapter Seven

Paperwork and Policies

Many would-be childminders are surprised by the sheer volume of paperwork that is involved with the service. Childminding paperwork falls into the following main groups:

- Formal documents providing proof of registration, insurance and qualifications and training.

- Policies and procedures.

- Records.

These are each covered in more detail throughout the following pages. It is best to approach the task of putting together the paperwork in a methodical way. A well-organised collection of well-written documents is one of the ways that you can demonstrate to parents and inspectors that you are able to provide a childminding service of the highest quality.

Specific requirements relating to England, Wales, Scotland and Northern Ireland are very similar but not identical. A range of recommended paperwork has been covered here but it is very important that you obtain specific current advice from the regulatory body for your area. Contact details are in the help list.

'Many would-be childminders are surprised by the sheer volume of paperwork that is involved with the service.'

Formal documents and certificates

Registration certificate

This is a very important document and should be displayed clearly in the premises where you are childminding so that parents can easily see it. The obvious solution is to frame it and hang it on the wall!

Public liability insurance

All childminders should have adequate insurance in respect of liability which may be incurred by them in the event of death, injury, public liability, damage or other loss occurring in relation to their childminding. You will need to present your insurance certificate at some point during your regular inspections. There are specific policies available to childminders. One such policy is available from the National Childminding Association (see the help list).

Car documents

If you intend transporting the children that you are caring for around in a vehicle, you will need to check that your motor vehicle insurance covers you for doing this by contacting your insurer. A valid MOT certificate is also needed to demonstrate that the vehicle has been passed as roadworthy. You may wish to obtain parents' written consent for transporting their children in your car.

Qualifications and training

You should put together a pack of all the certificates that you are awarded for the training that you complete. These would include your paediatric first-aid certificate, any pre-registration training that you have attended and any further training, e.g. to work with children with special needs. Training for childminders is dealt with in more detail in chapter 9.

Criminal Records Bureau checks

This includes the number and date of issue of the enhanced Criminal Records Bureau (CRB) disclosure, in respect of all people who work directly with children or who are likely to have unsupervised access to them.

Policies and procedures

What are policies and procedures?

A policy is a written statement about how you will work relating to a specific area of your service (i.e. what you aim to do). A procedure is a clear description of the actions that you will take to put the policy into practice (i.e. how you will do it). They are a way of you demonstrating that you have considered a particular issue carefully and worked out a way of dealing with it.

Policies do not have to be long or complicated; in fact, the best policies are often short, simple and clear.

Procedures can be set out as a checklist of what you will do and when and how you will do it.

Can I get help to write them?

Many policies and procedures have to be submitted as part of your application process or inspected during your pre-registration inspection. Help and guidance is available in pre-registration training. Also, the NCMA has sample policies and procedures that their members can download and adapt to their own service (see the help list for contact details). However, it is still your responsibility to make the policy relevant to your own situation and to review it regularly.

What do I do once I've written them?

Policies are not just written and forgotten about. The date that they are written should be recorded on them as well as the date when they are due to be reviewed.

Reviews can also be prompted if you try to use the procedure in a particular situation and find that it does not work; following feedback from parents or after changes in national guidance.

'A procedure is a clear description of the actions that you will take to put the policy into practice (i.e. how you will do it).'

A section can be entered at the bottom of the policy where parents can sign to confirm that they have read and understood them. If you have anyone else working with you they must also be familiar with the policies and procedures in place.

The National Childminding Association has produced sample policies and procedures for their members to use. The most common policies associated with childminding are as follows in alphabetical order.

Accident policy and procedure

An accident and emergency policy includes a policy statement about accidents involving the children in your care, your own children and yourself. It could include statements about your first-aid training; details about the first-aid facilities that you have and parents' emergency contact details.

'Policies are not just written and forgotten about.'

The procedure is a clear plan of action to follow in the case of an accident and details of emergency back-up cover. The need to record accidents and bring them to the attention of parents should also be outlined. See the accident records section later in this chapter.

Alcohol policy

A statement that no one under the influence of alcohol will have contact with children in your care.

Behaviour policy and procedure

A behaviour policy is a clear statement of your approach to promoting appropriate behaviour. The procedure is a list of how you will promote appropriate behaviour in practice including how you will involve parents; how you will re-enforce positive behaviour; the sanctions that you will use and when those sanctions will be introduced.

Complaints policy and procedure

A complaints policy is a clear statement of your positive attitude towards complaints, how complaints can be made and how you will deal with them. The procedure is a list of the steps that you will take when dealing with a complaint, including investigating it (with time limits), reporting it to the appropriate regulatory authority and recording it.

Confidentiality policy and procedure

A confidentiality policy is a clear statement about how you will protect and securely manage personal information about the families you work with. The procedure includes a description of all the personal information that you hold; how you keep it secure and the procedures for releasing that information.

Crèche policy and procedure

A crèche policy is a clear statement of the circumstances under which you would use a crèche (daycare) for the children in your care, for example, while you attend a training course. The procedure includes the way in which parents' prior permission for this will be sought; checks that you will make on the crèche before children are placed there and time limits for the children being in the crèche.

Food and drink policy and procedure

A food and drink policy is a clear statement of your aim to provide healthy and nutritious food and drink to the children in your care. The procedure is a description of the ways that you will go about ensuring that the food that you provide is safe (food hygiene), healthy (nutritional) and interesting (variety) and also takes into account individual dietary requirements as indicated by the parents. Further information on food safety is given later in this chapter.

Fire safety risk assessment and procedure for the emergency evacuation of the premises

A thorough assessment of fire risks at the premises and the procedure to get all staff and children out safely should a fire occur. This may have to include a plan of the premises.

Illness policy and procedure

'An illness policy is a clear statement of your intention to promote good health and prevent the spread of infections among the children you care for.'

An illness policy is a clear statement of your intention to promote good health and prevent the spread of infections among the children you care for. The procedure is the way in which you will achieve this by acting appropriately when a child becomes ill and is suspected of having an infectious disease. This includes excluding children with specific diseases from your childcare service for periods specified by Health Authority Guidance. Guidance on exclusion policies can be obtained from the Health Protection Agency website (www.hpa.org.uk). It is good practice to have these available and make parents aware of them so there can be no misunderstanding when a child is ill. A contact number for your local HPA office so that you can seek urgent advice is also useful. You should also include your general hygiene precautions relating to changing nappies and toileting children and hand washing. Hygiene procedures for any pets that are present at the home should also be included.

Inclusion or equal opportunities policy and procedure

An inclusion policy is a clear statement about your aim to ensure that an inclusive attitude is shown to all users of your service and that you will challenge discriminatory behaviour. The procedure will set out how you will include this in your equipment, activities, resources, records and procedures. This ranges from having books and toys that reflect a positive image of all genders, ethnicity and religion, to your ability in dealing with and challenging a racist or discriminatory remark that is made by a child or a parent. This will include the ways that you will support children with special educational needs and/or disabilities.

Lost child policy and procedure

The policy is a clear statement about supervision of children on outings. The procedure will include a list of precautions to make sure that a child does not get lost (having a pre-outing activity with the children emphasising that they should be aware of where you are, not wander off and what to do if they become lost). It will also set out the action that you will take if a child goes missing (i.e. informing responsible adults at the venue, e.g. security guards or stewards) or informing the police if it is in an open place and of course informing the parents.

Medicines policy and procedure

A medicines policy is a clear statement of your aim to have an effective, safe procedure that meets the individual needs of each child when administering medicines. Your procedure would include reference to:

- Records of all medicines administered.

- Safe storage of medicine.

- Written permission from parents for administering medicine.

- Training you may require to administer special medicines.

Outings policy and procedure

An outings policy is a clear statement of the value of outings for children and your aim to keep children safe whilst on outings. Your procedure would include details of:

- Ratios of adults to children required on outings.

- Trial runs and risk assessments of outings.

- How written parental permission for outings will be obtained.

- The records and equipment that you will take on outings.

- The use of car seats.

- A link to the policies and procedures covering accidents and a lost child.

Safeguarding children policy and procedure

A safeguarding children policy is a clear statement indicating that you understand your responsibilities with regard to the safety of all children in your care. Also, a clear statement that you will report any concerns that you have regarding a child's safety and welfare to the appropriate authorities. The statement also indicates that you are aware that it is your duty to notify your regulatory body of any allegations of abuse. The procedure sets out:

- That you will keep up-to-date with child protection issues by attending appropriate training.
- That you will make sure that you have up-to-date literature from your regulatory authority and from NCMA on this issue.
- That you will put together a safe procedure for releasing a child to an unknown person if the parent cannot collect them e.g. by the use of a password.
- What you will do if you think a child is being abused.
- The records that you will keep relating to child protection allegations against yourself or anyone else.

'A safeguarding children policy is a clear statement indicating that you understand your responsibilities with regard to the safety of all children in your care.'

Smoking policy and procedure

A smoking policy is a clear statement of your aim to provide a smoke-free environment for children. The procedure sets out how you will achieve this by making sure that no one smokes inside your home or in any of the outdoor spaces used by the children.

Staff recruitment and training policy

If you employ any staff to work with you, you will need a clear statement that you will ensure that they are suitable to work with the children in your care. Your procedure will set out the checks that you will follow before they can start work with you (including notifying the regulatory authority so they can carry out checks) and the ways in which you will ensure that the staff are trained and supervised appropriately.

Statement of aims and objectives

Clear statements about your aims and objectives for the delivery of your service.

Working with parents policy and procedure

A working with parents policy is a clear statement about your aim to work in partnership with parents to ensure that the needs of the child are met. The procedure will set out that you will achieve this by:

- Undergoing training and reading up-to-date guidance and literature about how this can be achieved.
- Making sure that parents have copies of all your policies and procedures.
- Agreeing a written contract with the parents before the child starts in your care.
- Reviewing contracts as regularly as needed.
- Setting out how payments must be made and when receipts will be issued.
- Holding regular reviews with parents and updating records.
- Establishing a method for parents to provide feedback on your service.
- Including parents in the inspection process so that they can make their views known and see the inspection report.

Uncollected child policy and procedure

The policy is a clear statement that you will continue to care for the child while the procedure is being followed. The procedure will clearly set out the action that you will take if a child is not collected within a specified time (e.g. one hour) of their nominated collection time. There will be a hierarchy of action ranging from attempting to contact the parents and other emergency contacts by telephone to contacting the duty social worker at your local authority. The relevant emergency numbers will be included.

Records

Some blank record books e.g. 'Accident books' are available to purchase from stationers and from the NCMA. It is recommended that all the following records are kept for three years from the date on which the information was recorded. They should be readily available for inspection by the regulatory authority.

Record of complaints

The records would include the date, the name of the person making the complaint, details of the complaint and how it was investigated and resolved. Any amendments to policies and procedures that were made as a result of the complaint should also be recorded.

'A record of risk assessments, clearly stating when they were carried out, by whom, the date of review and any action taken following a review or incident should be recorded and kept.'

Record of all medicines administered to children

Medicine records should include:

- The date and circumstances of its administration.
- Who it was administered by.
- A record of a parent's consent.

Record of accidents and first-aid treatment

A record of how the accident occurred, the injuries sustained and medical treatment administered.

Records relating to each of the children in your care

The following information is required:

- Full name.
- Date of birth.
- Name and address of every parent and carer who is known to the provider.

- Which parents or carers the child normally lives with.

- Emergency contact details of the parents and carers; alternative emergency contacts if the parents cannot be reached.

- A record of the name, home address and telephone number of the provider and any other person living or employed on the premises.

- A record of the name, home address and telephone number of anyone who will regularly be in unsupervised contact with the children.

- Persons who will collect the child if the parents can't.

- Child's medical details and doctor.

- Cultural or religious information that the parents wish you to take note of, allergies, special health requirements, special educational needs.

Attendance records

A daily record of the names of the children looked after on the premises and their hours of attendance.

Risk assessments on outings

A record of risk assessments, clearly stating when they were carried out, by whom, the date of review and any action taken following a review or incident should be recorded and kept. A risk assessment must be carried out for each specific outing with the children.

Summing Up

- Childminders are required to maintain a large amount of paperwork as part of their childminding service. The paperwork will be looked at during inspection and so an organised and methodical approach is needed.

- The paperwork falls into three categories. They are: formal documents, policies and procedures, and records.

- The formal documents are certificates and insurance documents relating to your service.

- The policies are written statements about how you will work relating to a specific area of your service.

- The procedures are generally checklists of the actions that you will take to carry out the policy.

- The policy and procedures relate to adverse events such as accidents and lost children and to ongoing issues such as behaviour.

- The records relate to day-to-day activities such as attendance and medicines administered.

- All paperwork must be kept up to date and regularly reviewed.

- You will be given help to write policies and procedures in pre-registration training. Help and sample documents are also available from the NCMA.

Chapter Eight

Running the Business

What will it cost me to get started?

This is very variable. If you already have pre-school aged children you may already have most of the toys and safety equipment that you will need. The costs of training and registration also vary. You may have to spend money on:

- Registration fees.
- Pre-registration training and first-aid training.
- Security check fees.
- NCMA membership.
- Public liability insurance.
- Paperwork.
- Alterations to your property such as additional fencing and gates.
- Equipment – toys, books, high chairs, smoke alarms, stairgates, fireguards, fire blankets, etc.

'In some areas, grants are available for new childminders to help set up their new business.'

Can I get any financial help to set up the business?

In some areas, grants are available for new childminders to help set up their new business. You can find out about these during your pre-registration briefing and from the NCMA.

How do I find clients?

Once you are registered and ready to start caring for children you will obviously need to ensure that parents know about the services that you provide and choose you as their childminder.

There are several ways to advertise your service.

Family Information Services

Your local Family Information Service will hold details on all registered childcare in your area. Ensure that they have your details and that those details are kept up to date. Many FIS websites have a childcare search facility where parents can specify a childcare type (i.e. childminding) and a geographical area by entering a postcode and a certain number of miles around that postcode (range). A list of providers is given. Childminders can enter brief details here about the service that they provide, including:

- Name, address, contact number and email.
- Your website address if you have one (see below).
- Your session times and limitations (e.g. term-time only).
- The age range of children that you can care for.
- Any details of your service (e.g. able to care for children with special needs).
- Your vacancies.
- Your charges (usually quoted per hour).
- The schools and nurseries that you pick up and drop off at or an area that you can do school/nursery pick-ups in.
- Details of your training, activities (e.g. the names of the local playgroups or soft play sessions that you attend) and facilities (e.g. large garden).

Your own website

This is obviously a good marketing strategy for you to use but will have to be balanced against the costs of setting up and maintaining a website which vary greatly.

A website will give you the space to properly describe your services and give parents all the information that they seek when they are choosing childcare. They will be interested to see information about:

* You – Your training and experience.
* Your facilities such as outdoor play space, vegetable patches, indoor play areas illustrated with photographs.
* More details about the hours that you are willing to work, your policies about bank holidays, etc.
* Your policies on payments, fees and deposits.
* Some examples of how you deliver the prescribed early learning policies for your area.
* An example of a typical day at your home.
* Your policies on providing food and snacks. How you cater for different dietary requirements and children with allergies. You can provide sample weekly menus.

Childcare search sites

There are dedicated search sites for parents looking for childcare. Most have search facilities where the parents can specify a type of childcare (i.e. childminding) and a postcode or area. It is generally free for childminders to register and to set up a simple profile where you can submit a photograph and some brief details about the services you offer. However, parents have to register in order to obtain your contact details and they are charged for this registration. Parents can read references that other parents have entered on your profile. There are often community areas and chat rooms.

'A website will give you the space to properly describe your services and give parents all the information that they seek when they are choosing childcare.'

Local advertising

You can put up a small (postcard-sized) advertisement in many newsagents and post offices. Other locations where people with young families gather may also allow you to display cards, e.g. leisure centres or community centres. Some childminders put advertising posters up in their cars.

Word of mouth

Some schools and children's centres have vacancy co-ordinators helping parents to find childminders with vacancies. If you network with other childminders, they can pass your details on to parents who enquire about places that they cannot provide.

Money matters

'You are self-employed and so it is up to you to charge what you wish.'

Can I choose what fees to charge?

Yes, you are self-employed and so it is up to you to charge what you wish. Obviously, if you set your fees too low, you will not make much money and parents may suspect that you offer an inferior service because you're so cheap!

On the other hand, if you charge too much, you will not be able to compete with other childminders in your area.

How do I charge for my service?

Most childminders charge by the hour but others charge a daily or weekly fee. Some charge more for part-time places than full-time. You may wish to charge different rates for school holidays or weekends or for care provided outside of the normal hours, e.g. later at night or earlier in the morning. You may offer discounts to siblings. This is entirely your decision but you must be absolutely clear about your charges and agree them in advance with parents so that no misunderstandings or disagreements occur.

Obviously you will earn more money the more children you care for; however, your registration will limit the number of children of particular ages that you can care for. You will also earn more money the longer hours you work but you will have to balance this with the needs of your own family. Find out what other childminders in your geographical area are charging and go from there.

What is the average fee?

In 2011, NCMA childminders in England and Wales charged an average of £3.71 per child per hour, but the rates varied regionally. The average fees charged by childminders in Greater London were £5.02, whereas fees in West Midlands averaged £3.36 per child per hour.

How will I receive payment?

Childminders are paid by cash, cheque, by BACS, or by childcare vouchers. These arrangements will need to be made at the time that you start caring for the child and setting up the contract.

How do childcare vouchers work?

Employees of some companies can choose to receive a portion of their salary as childcare vouchers. This has advantages for both the employee (as a parent) and the employer. The parent does not have to pay tax or national insurance contributions on the first portion. The employer also reduces their national insurance contribution and benefits from reduced short-term absenteeism, and the scheme attracts more people back to work once they have become parents. Companies called Childcare Voucher Providers may administer the schemes for employers.

Which parents will be eligible?

Employees are eligible to be paid through the scheme if:

- Their employer offers it.

- They have a bank account.

- They are using a registered childcarer (including registered childminders).

- The carer is not a relative (unless they care for other children as well).

What do I do with the vouchers?

- Online accounts – The value of the voucher is credited to the online account of the employee. Regular or ad hoc payments can then be made electronically to the childcare provider.

- Paper vouchers – You have to redeem the paper vouchers by post, telephone, online or direct with the childcare voucher provider.

- Automated vouchers – Where a fixed regular amount is paid to a childcare provider, a standing order type arrangement can be set up. This requires less administration from yourself. You will be sent a remittance advice when a payment is made.

Tax and national insurance

You will need to register as self-employed with Her Majesty's Revenue and Customs (HMRC). You will need to keep accurate and up-to-date records of income and expenditure. More help is available from NCMA and HMRC (see the help list).

Contracts

It is vital to have contracts agreed with the parents of all the children you care for. Contracts do not just specify charges but ensure that everyone knows what will happen about issues such as bank holidays; about family holidays; when you or the child are ill; times for collection and how payments must be made. The NCMA have template contracts that members can use (see the help list for contact details).

A typical day

The thing that attracts many people to a childminding career is that no two days are the same! Having said that, there will be certain routines (e.g. sleeping and eating) and commitments (e.g. school pick-ups) that will dictate a certain order to your day. Some childminders advertise typical timetables on their websites. They usually include the following:

- Drop-off and settling in periods.
- School/nursery drop-off for older children.
- Free play.
- Snack times.
- Structured activities.
- Lunch time.
- Outdoor play.
- Quiet play or nap time.
- School/nursery pick-ups.
- Home time.

Registering as a food business

As a childminder, you may have to register as a food business with your local authority.

How do I know if I should register?

The Food Standards Agency has produced specific advice to help you decide if you should register. In summary, if you only do the following, you do not need to register:

- Provide mains water as a drink.
- Provide plates, bowls and cutlery for the children to eat their own packed lunches.

'The thing that attracts many people to a childminding career is that no two days are the same!'

- Provide chilled storage (a fridge) for children to store their packed lunches.

- Help the children eat their packed lunch (e.g. cutting up food) if they need it.

- 'Occasionally' provide food but not as part of your regular service. This would include a cake to celebrate a child's birthday or feeding the child in an emergency situation when the parent has not been able to collect them.

If I do need to register, what should I do?

You will need to register with your local authority food safety department. You can find out how to contact them by using the search facility on the Food Standards Agency website at: http://www.food.gov.uk/enforcement/enforceessential/yourarea/.

'As a childminder, you may have to register as a food business with your local authority.'

Your food safety department will tell you exactly how to register in your area but it is likely to involve completing a form online or in paper about contact and address details and the type of food business (i.e. childminding) that you have.

Will I have a food safety inspection?

Yes, a food safety officer from the local authority will call to inspect your premises and to discuss food hygiene matters with you. However, the officer will be aware that the premises is also your home and will be able to advise on food hygiene whilst taking this into account.

Are there any specific hygiene tips for childminders?

Yes, whether you have to register or not, you should be aware of hygiene issues that could affect the children in your care. The main ones are as follows:

Pet hygiene

It's very common to have pets in homes that are used for childminding and they can be of great benefit to the children as a way of learning about animals and how to care for them correctly. However, if pets are allowed in food preparation areas or areas where children eat their food, they can introduce harmful microorganisms that could make the children ill. To control this effectively, pet access to areas where food is prepared or served should be carefully controlled. Pets should not be allowed on food preparation surfaces. If a pet has been on a food preparation surface or been in contact with any utensils they must be thoroughly cleaned and disinfected before food is prepared/eaten.

Nappy changing

Baby nappy changing should be carried out away from areas where food is prepared or eaten. Soiled nappies should be disposed of quickly and never left on food preparation surfaces. A strict routine for hand washing and disinfecting the changing surface after changing nappies must be followed.

Washing machines

It is common for domestic washing machines to be found in the kitchen. Where this is the case, make sure that you follow a strict routine that does not allow soiled clothing to come into contact with food preparation surfaces. If this does happen, clean and disinfect the surface thoroughly.

General hygiene

Hand washing is an essential part of food hygiene for all childminders and the children they care for. Make regular hand washing part of your routine. In particular, hands should be washed:

- Before handling and eating food (including snacks).
- After touching raw meat or vegetables.

- After using the toilet or changing nappies.
- After putting out the rubbish.
- After doing the laundry.
- After touching pets.
- After outdoor play.

Do I have to go on a food hygiene course?

As a childminder, you are not required to attend a formal food hygiene course. However, it would be beneficial and useful when marketing your business.

Do I need to keep any paperwork relating to food hygiene?

The Food Standards Agency has produced specific food safety guidance for childminders. When you are visited by a food safety officer they will be making reference to this pack so it is a good idea to study it and put it into practice.

It contains eight safe method sheets and a diary for you to personalise. It is a way of you demonstrating that you have safe systems in place for food hygiene and is based on the hazard analysis critical control point (HACCP) approach that is required by law.

The method sheets relate to the main elements of food hygiene namely: cross-contamination, cleaning, chilling and cooking.

The diary contains 'action sheets' and '3-monthly review' sheets. The pack is well set out and easy to follow.

'As a childminder, you are not required to attend a formal food hygiene course. However, it would be beneficial and useful when marketing your business.'

Summing Up

- There are some initial costs involved in setting up a childminding service. These relate to insurance, registration fees, security checks and maybe some equipment or alterations to your premises.

- In some areas you can access grants to help you get started. You can get details during your pre-registration briefing and from the NCMA.

- You can advertise for clients using the Family Information Service, your own website, childcare search sites or local advertising.

- You can choose the way that you want to charge for your service and how much you charge. It is a good idea to find out what other childminders in your area are charging before you set your fees.

- You will receive payment as cheque, cash, bank transfer or childcare vouchers.

- You will have to notify HMRC that you are receiving income as a self-employed person and follow their advice.

- You may also have to register as a food business.

- There are specific hygiene arrangements that childminders should follow relating to pets, changing nappies, dirty laundry and hand washing.

Chapter Nine
Training and Career Opportunities

Paediatric first-aid training

A current qualification in first aid is a requirement of registration in most areas of the UK and highly recommended for all childminders. The general advice is that if you are caring for children below the age of puberty, a specific paediatric qualification is required. Some childminders may care for children above the age of puberty (e.g. a child with special needs) and they may be required to attend adult first-aid training.

It is important to update your training on a regular basis.

Childminders should ensure that the training:

- Is suitable for practitioners that are caring for children in the absence of their parents.

- Is a minimum of 12 hours long.

- Covers what should be included in a first-aid kit for babies and children.

- Demonstrates resuscitation techniques using models of babies and children and gives them a chance to practise on models of each age group.

- Includes how to record accidents and incidents appropriately.

Your local authority and Family Information Service will be able to advise you on appropriate locally run courses.

'A current qualification in first aid is a requirement of registration in most areas of the UK and highly recommended for all childminders.'

What is pre-registration basic training?

Recent changes introduced by Ofsted from September 2012, mean that now all childminders must undertake local authority approved training before they can register with Ofsted. Previously, childminders had six months after registering to complete this training. Prospective childminders must contact their local authority or Family Information Service to check which introductory courses they approve as this may vary between areas and changes are being introduced all the time.

The NCMA offers training that covers the essentials of starting up and running a childminding service. It is called 'Understanding How to Set Up a Home-Based Childcare Service'. It is also referred to as the COYPOP5. It covers the basic information that you need to start up a childminding service and comprises of seven units. They are:

'It is highly recommended (and required in some areas) that childminders take basic training before they set up in business.'

Unit 1: Understand how to set up a home-based childcare service.

- Current legislation and the role of regulatory bodies.

- How to develop the necessary policies and procedures.

- The importance of confidentiality and data protection.

- Marketing.

- Financial planning.

- Sources of support and information.

Unit 2: Understand how to establish a safe and healthy home-based environment for children.

- The key components of a healthy and safe home-based environment.

- The principles of safe supervision of children on and off site.

- Suitability and safety of equipment.

- How to obtain current guidance on health and safety risk assessment of the home-based work setting.

- Storage and administration of medicines.

Unit 3: Understand the importance of partnerships with parents for all aspects of the home-based childcare service.

* The importance of partnerships with parents.

* How partnerships with parents are set up and maintained.

Unit 4: Understand the principles of development of routines for home-based childcare.

* How routines are based on the child's needs, agreements with parents and involve the participation of children.

* Adapting routines to meet the needs of children of different ages and stages of development.

* How to ensure that each child is welcomed and valued.

Unit 5: Understand how to provide play and other activities for children in home-based settings that will support equality and inclusion.

* The importance of play to children's learning and development and the need for an inclusive approach.

* How to plan a challenging and enjoyable learning environment in the home that includes using everyday domestic routines and household items.

* What can be learned about children by observing them at play.

* How and why it is important that children receive equal treatment and access, based on their individual needs and acknowledging their rights.

* Compare how other resources available for children support their play.

Unit 6: Understand how home-based childcarers can support the safeguarding of children in their care.

* The concept of safeguarding and the duty of care that applies to all practitioners.

* The possible signs, symptoms, indicators and behaviours that may cause concern in the context of safeguarding.

- The regulatory requirements for safeguarding children that affect home-based childcare.

- The procedures that need to be followed by lone workers in home-based settings when harm or abuse are suspected or alleged, either against them or third parties.

Unit 7: Understand the principles of supporting positive behaviour in home-based childcare settings.

- The typical behaviours exhibited by children linked to their stage of development and key events in their lives.

- How ground rules for behaviour and expectations are developed and implemented.

'There are several options for further training for childminders.'

How can I access the pre-registration training?

The courses are sometimes delivered face-to-face over a number of sessions by a partnership of the NCMA and a local authority. In Wales, NCMA Cymru can deliver the course on behalf of local authorities. It takes 14 hours in total and is assessed through a multiple choice questionnaire at the end of the course. This is the recommended route to accessing the course in Wales.

It can also be accessed as an individual via e-learning. The advantage of e-learning is that you can do the course at your own pace and at times that suit you. However, some people prefer the support provided by a face-to-face course that also allows you to meet other prospective childminders.

A textbook is provided with the course and there are assignments to complete electronically. All learners have access to extra skills for life training as well.

What about further training?

There are several options for further training for childminders.

Need2Know

Diploma

There is a level 3 diploma called 'The Diploma for the Children and Young People's Workforce'. It has been developed for all people involved in the care of children and young people. The diploma is made up of several units. Some units are mandatory and then you can select the remaining units that are most appropriate to your career. By the end of the diploma you must have achieved 65 credits.

You can get more information from the NCMA, your local authority and local colleges and career advice centres.

Foundation degree

Foundation degrees are level 5 qualifications which are another training option for you to consider. Many are very suitable for childminders and include:

* Early Childhood Studies.
* Early Years Childcare and Education.
* Working with Children (Early Years).
* Early Years Senior Practitioner.

Unlike some other degree courses, you do not necessarily have to have formal qualifications to get on to them. Your professional childcare experience as well as your previous childcare qualifications will be taken into account. Many childminders find foundation degrees particularly suitable for them because they require you to be working in the environment about which you are studying.

You can get more information from the NCMA, your local authority and local colleges and career advice centres.

Early Years Professional

Early Years Professionals (EYPs) are role models to other people working in the early years workforce, acting as change agents and leading and supporting others to improve practice.

Childminders can become EYPs, underlining the professional position that childminders hold in the early years workforce.

To become an EYP you need to gain Early Years Professional status – a level 6 qualification – by demonstrating you meet a series of national graduate-level EYP standards in working with children up to five years of age.

For eligible candidates, all EYPS training pathways are fully funded.

The organisation co-ordinating training for Early Years Practitioners has recently changed. It is now possible to access information using a qualification finder facility on the Department for Education website https://www.education.gov.uk/eypqd/qualification-search.

Continuing professional development

As well as the compulsory training for childminders, it is highly recommended that they continue their training throughout their career, increasing their confidence and skills and offering a better service for the families they work with.

Local authorities and local branches of the NCMA hold one-day training sessions that can help give you new ideas and help you to extend the services you offer. These sessions cover subjects such as child protection or disability equality, or help extend experience in particular areas of play such as messy play.

Childminders who belong to quality-assured childminding networks often have access to extra training organised by their network co-ordinators.

These could include:

* Child protection.
* Equal opportunites and inclusion.
* Special educational needs.
* Early Years Foundation Stage.
* Reflective practice.
* Marketing.

'Local authorities and local branches of the NCMA hold one-day training sessions that can help give you new ideas and help you to extend the services you offer.'

- The business side of childminding.

- Working with vulnerable children.

- Foundation Phase (in Wales).

What about child protection training?

The NCMA have a course that has been developed by the NSPCC. It covers the roles and responsibilities in safeguarding children and the good practice guidelines for recognising and reporting child abuse. This is an e-learning course, accessed via the internet from the NCMA website. You will receive a personalised certificate at the end of the course.

Food hygiene training

Many childminders choose to attend a basic food hygiene course. They are widely available and you will be given a certificate to prove that you have attended. Details of local courses are available from your local authority Food Safety Department or by doing a simple search online. Some courses are also available online (e.g. via the NCMA). This will be a way of demonstrating to parents that you are aware of food hygiene issues and know how to prepare food safely. A basic food hygiene course will teach you about:

- Germs and food poisoning.

- Personal hygiene.

- Clean as you go.

- Temperature control.

- Food preparation/cooking.

- General food safety.

What career opportunities are open to childminders?

Whilst the majority of childminders work in their own businesses caring for children, there are further opportunities if you want to pursue them. You could join with another childminder to form a partnership or you could employ staff to help you.

Many registered childminders have expertise in caring for disabled children. According to the NCMA's 2010 membership survey, more than a third of members have undertaken specific training into caring for disabled children and those with additional needs

The Early Years Team at your local authority often run community childminding networks. These networks provide respite care for families of disabled children and you will be paid by the local authority for doing this. The child's needs are likely to be complex and so one-to-one care is usually required. To reflect this, the hourly rate is higher than you would normally receive.

Some families choose to nominate their childminder for one of the awards that celebrate the best childcarers in the country. There are several awards with nominations accepted at different times during the year. These include:

- Pre-School Learning Alliance Play awards.
- 4Children Children Stars.
- Nursery World awards.
- Early Years Educator awards (Childminder of the Year category).

Summing Up

- All childminders should have an up-to-date paediatric first-aid certificate.

- Recent changes made by Ofsted to the way they will regulate and inspect childminding services mean that all childminders must undertake local authority approved training before they register with Ofsted. Your local authority can let you know which courses are approved in your area.

- Some training is delivered face-to-face and some can be accessed online.

- If you want to obtain further qualifications, there are opportunities for you to study for a diploma or degree in a childcare subject.

- When you are working as a childminder, your local childminding network or local branch of the NCMA can provide details of further training so that you can keep your skills up to date.

- Some childminders with special training choose to work for local authorities providing respite care for families of children with disabilities.

Chapter Ten

Additional Information

What are the checks for previous offences and the vetting and barring scheme?

In order to keep children safe, it was decided that people with certain previous offences would not be allowed to work in certain occupations that involved contact with children. One of these occupations was childminding, as childminders have frequent unsupervised contact with very young children.

The checks are required for yourself, anyone looking after children with you and other people aged 16 or over living or working on the premises where you intend to childmind. The checks involve filling out a form of authorisation and paying a fee.

You will see this system of checks referred to as 'The Vetting and Barring Scheme' and 'Criminal Records Bureau checks (CRB checks)' and 'Disclosure Scotland checks' and an 'Independent Safeguarding Authority registration number' is also referred to. It is very important to obtain up-to-date advice from your regulatory authority about which checks have to be carried out. They can supply you with the correct forms and advise you about what fee (if any) you will have to pay.

The system as it stands is now considered too complex and intrusive and so a review has been carried out. Changes are to be implemented during 2012. It is very important, therefore, to get the most up-to-date advice on what forms you have to complete from your regulatory authority during the registration stage.

How many children can I care for?

As part of the registration process, the inspector will make a decision about how many children you can care for at one time. If you employ an assistant you will normally be allowed to care for more children. There are some general guidelines for this that are outlined below but the final decision is always down to the regulating body. They will take into consideration factors such as the space available, type of premises, other children that you are responsible for (i.e. your own or other relatives) and whether the children are siblings.

In general, you can care for up to six children aged under eight years. Of these:

※ No more than three children may be aged from birth to 31st August following their fifth birthday.

※ There is a limit on how many of these can be very young children (i.e. aged under 18 months (Wales) or under 12 months (England).

In certain circumstances you may be allowed to:

※ Care for more than one child aged less than 12 months (e.g. twins).

※ Care for more than three children aged less than five years.

Care provided for children aged eight and over is not allowed to adversely affect the care provided for children aged less than eight years.

Children that you care for who are aged four and five and in full-time education may be counted as being in the later year's age group.

'In general, you can care for up to six children aged under eight years.'

Is there any reason why I should not apply to become a childminder?

The registration process is in place in order to check your ability and suitability for childminding. There are certain circumstances that will disqualify you from registering as a childminder. A full list can be found in the laws that govern childminding that are outlined at the start of chapters 2-5.

The circumstances involve committing offences against children and having a previous disqualification or cancellation of registration. If someone you live with is disqualified this automatically means that you are disqualified as well. So, it's very important to talk with partners and others in the household before making an application.

In some situations disqualification can be waived. You can discuss your personal circumstances confidentially with your regulatory authority before making an application.

Early Years Foundation Stage (England)

The Early Years Foundation Stage (EYFS) sets the standards that all early years providers, including childminders, must meet to ensure that children learn and develop well and are kept healthy and safe. It promotes teaching and learning to ensure that children are ready for school and gives them the broad range of knowledge and skills that provide the right foundation for good future progress through school and life.

'There are certain circumstances that will disqualify you from registering as a childminder.'

Learning and development

These requirements define what providers must do, working in partnership with parents and/or carers, to promote the learning and development of all children in their care, and to ensure they are ready for school. The learning and development requirements have been put together using the best available evidence on how children learn and reflect the broad range of skills, knowledge and attitudes children need.

The learning and development requirements comprise:

- The seven areas of learning and development and the educational programmes which are: communication and language; physical development; personal, social and emotional development; literacy; mathematics; understanding the world and creative arts and design.

- The early learning goals, which summarise the knowledge, skills and understanding that all young children should have gained by the end of the Reception year.

- The assessment requirements (when and how practitioners must assess children's achievements, and when and how they should discuss children's progress with parents and/or carers).

Safeguarding and welfare

It is recognised that children learn best when they are healthy, safe and secure, when their individual needs are met and when they have positive relationships with the adults caring for them. The safeguarding and welfare requirements of the Early Years Foundation Stage are designed to help providers create high-quality settings which are welcoming, safe and stimulating, and where children are able to enjoy learning and grow in confidence.

Childminders are required to take all necessary steps to keep children safe and well. They must safeguard children; ensure the suitability of adults who have contact with children; promote good health; manage behaviour and maintain records, policies and procedures.

Changes to the EYFS

A revised and simplified framework for the Early Years Foundation Stage (EYFS) was published on 27th March 2012. It was implemented in September 2012.

The revised framework aims to free professionals from bureaucracy so that they can focus on supporting children, and is part of a wider strategy of removing regulation and paperwork.

The key changes are summarised below.

Areas of learning and development

This now consists of three prime areas and four specific areas. The prime areas cover the knowledge and skills which are the foundations for children's school readiness and future progress, and which are applied and reinforced by the specific areas. The literacy and maths sections form baselines for the National Curriculum.

Early learning goals and assessment

Instead of 69 goals, there are now 17 against which judgements are made. For each goal, assessors determine whether children are meeting expected levels, are exceeding them, or are below the expected level ('emerging'). Providers are required to share the report on each child, along with a brief report on the characteristics of learning, with the Year 1 teacher.

Progress check at age two

The revised Early Years Foundation Stage introduces a requirement for providers to review children's progress when a child is aged between two and three. A short written summary must be provided to parents or carers, highlighting achievements and areas in which extra support might be needed, and describing how the provider will address any issues.

Play and teaching

It is has been made clearer that providers are responsible for ongoing judgements about the balance between play and teaching, between activities led by children and activities led or guided by adults.

English as an additional language

The relevant requirements give clearer focus on the reasonable steps providers must take, including the assessment of children's skills in English.

Wrap-around and holiday care

The framework now makes clear that the EYFS requirements do not need to be delivered in full when children spend limited amounts of time in a setting.

'The revised Early Years Foundation Stage introduces a requirement for providers to review children's progress when a child is aged between two and three.'

Child protection

Examples of adults' behaviour which might be signs of abuse and neglect are included. If they become aware of any such signs, staff should respond appropriately in order to safeguard children.

Safeguarding policies and procedures must cover the use of mobile phones and cameras in the setting.

Suitable people

The requirements for providers to check the suitability of managers have been simplified. Providers will be responsible for obtaining criminal record disclosures on managers.

Staff qualifications, training, support and skills

A requirement has been introduced in relation to staff supervision. Providers must give staff opportunities for coaching and training, mutual support, teamwork, continuous improvement and confidential discussion of sensitive issues.

Childminders will be required to complete local authority approved training in the Early Years Foundation Stage before they register with Ofsted.

Staff:child ratios

There is a clarification of the circumstances in which there may be exceptions to the staff:child ratios for childminders caring for children of mixed ages.

Safety and suitability of premises, environment and equipment

The requirements in relation to risk assessment have been adjusted to clarify that it is for providers to judge whether a risk assessment needs to be recorded.

Themes and principles of the Early Years Foundation Stage 2012

The document *Development Matters in the Early Years Foundation Stage* is non-statutory guidance material produced by 'The British Association for Early Childhood Education'. It gives guidance on the four themes of the Early Years Foundation Stage. The themes are summarised below.

Theme: Unique child.

Principle: Every child is a unique child who is constantly learning and can be resilient, capable, confident and self-assured.

Practice: Practitioners should:

- Understand and observe each child's development and learning, assess progress and plan for next steps.
- Support babies and children to develop a positive sense of their own identity and culture.
- Identify any need for additional support.
- Keep children safe.
- Value and respect all children and families equally.

Theme: Positive relationships

Principle: Children learn to be strong and independent through positive relationships.

Practice: Positive relationships should be:

- Warm and loving and foster a sense of belonging.
- Sensitive and responsive to the child's needs, feelings and interests.
- Supportive of the child's own efforts and independence.

- Consistent in setting clear boundaries.
- Stimulating.
- Built on key person relationships.

Theme: Enabling environments

Principle: Children learn and develop well in enabling environments, in which their experiences respond to their individual needs and there is a strong partnership between parents and practitioner.

Practice: Enabling environments:

- Value all people.
- Value learning.
- Offer stimulating resources that are relevant to all the children's cultures and communities.
- Offer rich learning opportunities through play and playful teaching.
- Offer support for children to take risks and explore.

Theme: Learning and development

Principle: Children develop and learn in different ways. The framework covers the education and care of all children in early years provision, including children with special educational needs and disabilities.

Practice: Practitioners should:

- Teach children by ensuring challenging, playful opportunities across the prime and specific areas of learning and development.
- Foster the characteristics of effective early learning (playing and exploring, active learning and creating and thinking critically).

Summing Up

- Before you can register as a childminder, security checks will need to be carried out on you and anyone over 16 years of age that lives with you. These checks are to protect children.

- The laws relating to these checks are being changed so it is very important that you get up-to-date advice from your regulatory authority.

- As part of your registration you will be told the maximum number of children that you can care for. You are not normally allowed to care for more than six children under the age of eight years old.

- There are certain circumstances that will disqualify you from becoming a childminder. It is important to establish that these do not apply to you or anyone in your household before you commence the registration process.

- As a prospective childminder you should be familiar with the four themes of the Early Years Foundation Stage which are: unique child; positive relationships; enabling environments and learning and development.

- Childminders must also be familiar with the learning and development and welfare and safeguarding requirements.

- Recent changes have been made to the Early Years Foundation Stage requirements in England. The changes aim to reduce paperwork and regulation.

Help List

Early Years Resources

BBC – Schools: Early Years Foundation Stage

Website: www.bbc.co.uk/schools/websites/eyfs/
Ideas and resources for delivering the Early Years Foundation Stage.

Foundation Years: From Pregnancy to Children Aged 5

Website: www.foundationyears.org.uk/
A very useful website packed with resources, information and the latest news relating to the Early Years Foundation Stage.

Organisations providing information for childminders

Food Standards Agency

For food hygiene advice, advice on whether you should register as a food business and up-to-date information on food safety. Contact the Food Safety Department of your local council and the Food Standards Agency.

Food Standards Agency, UK Headquarters,
Aviation House, 125 Kingsway, London WC2B 6NH
Tel: 020 7276 8000 (switchboard)
Email: helpline@foodstandards.gsi.gov.uk
Website: www.food.gov.uk

Food Standards Agency in Wales,
11th Floor, Southgate House, Wood Street, Cardiff, CF10 1EW
Tel: 02920 678999
Email: wales@foodstandards.gsi.gov.uk
Website: www.food.gov.uk

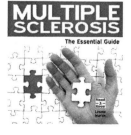